OLD MO

HOROSCOPE AND ASTRAL DIARY

GEMINI

foulsham
LONDON • NEW YORK • TORONTO • SYDNEY

foulsham

Capital Point, 33 Bath Road, Slough, Berkshire, SL1 3UF, England

Foulsham books can be found in all good bookshops and direct from
www.foulsham.com

ISBN: 978-0-572-04406-0

A CIP record for this book is available from the British Library

Printed and bound by CPI Group (UK) Ltd, Croydon, CR0 4YY.

CONTENTS

INTRODUCTION

Astrology has been a part of life for centuries now, and no matter how technological our lives become, it seems that it never diminishes in popularity. For thousands of years people have been gazing up at the star clad heavens and seeing their own activities and proclivities reflected in the movement of those little points of light. Across centuries countless hours have been spent studying the way our natures, activities and decisions seem to be paralleled by their predictable movements. Old Moore, a time-served veteran in astrological research, continues to monitor the zodiac and has produced the Astral Diary for 2014, tailor-made to your own astrological makeup.

Old Moore's Astral Diary is unique in its ability to get the heart of your nature and to offer you the sort of advice that might come from a trusted friend. It enables you to see in a day-by-day sense exactly how the planets are working for you. The diary section advises how you can get the best from upcoming situations and allows you to plan ahead successfully. There's also room on each daily entry to record your own observations or appointments.

While other popular astrology books merely deal with your astrological 'Sun sign', the Astral Diaries go much further. Every person on the planet is unique and Old Moore allows you to access your individuality in a number of ways. The front section gives you the chance to work out the placement of the Moon at the time of your birth and to see how its position has set an important seal on your overall nature. Perhaps most important of all, you can use the Astral Diary to discover your Rising Sign. This is the zodiac sign that was appearing over the Eastern horizon at the time of your birth and is just as important to you as an individual as is your Sun sign.

It is the synthesis of many different astrological possibilities that makes you what you are and with the Astral Diaries you can learn so much. How do you react to love and romance? Through the unique Venus tables and the readings that follow them, you can learn where the planet Venus was at the time of your birth. It is even possible to register when little Mercury is 'retrograde', which means that it appears to be moving backwards in space when viewed from the Earth. Mercury rules communication, so be prepared to deal with a few setbacks in this area when you see the sign ☿. The Astral Diary will be an interest and a support throughout the whole year ahead.

Old Moore extends his customary greeting to all people of the Earth and offers his age-old wishes for a happy and prosperous period ahead.

THE ESSENCE OF GEMINI

Exploring the Personality of Gemini the Twins

(22nd MAY – 21st JUNE)

What's in a sign?

When working at your best there isn't much doubt that you are one of the most popular people to be found anywhere in the zodiac. Why? Because you are bubbly, charming, full of fun and the perfect companion. But there's more to it than that. Your natural Mercurial charm could coax the birds down from the trees and you exude the sort of self-confidence that would convince almost anyone that you know exactly what you want, and how to go about getting it. Virtually any task you choose to undertake is done in a flash and when at your best you can remove more obstacles than a bulldozer.

So, you ask, if all this is true, why aren't I doing even better in life than I am? The simple fact is that beneath all the bravado and that oh-so-confident exterior is a small child, who is often lost and afraid in a world that can be complicated, large and threatening. If ever there was a person who epitomised a split personality, it surely has to be the typical Gemini subject. That impulsive, driving, Mercury-ruled enthusiasm simply insists on pushing you to the front of any queue, but once you are there the expectations of all those standing behind can begin to prey on your mind. This is why so many of your plans stall before they are brought to completion, and it also explains all those times that you simply run out of energy and virtually collapse into a heap. There is a lot to learn if you want to get the best out of what the zodiac has given you. Fortunately, life itself is your schoolyard and there is plenty you can do to make the very best of your natural talents.

Read through the following sections carefully, and when you have done so, get ready to put all your latent talents to the test. As you grow in confidence, so you will find that you are not as alone as you sometimes think. The keywords for the sign of Gemini are 'I think', but for you this isn't an insular process. Life itself is your launching pad to success and happiness – just as long as you learn to concentrate on the task at hand.

Gemini resources

The part of the zodiac occupied by the sign of Gemini has, for many centuries, been recognised as the home of communication. Almost everything that you are as an individual is associated with your need to keep in constant touch with the world at large. This trait is so marked that Geminis seem to dream more than most other people, so that even in your sleep the need to keep looking, talking and explaining is as essential to you as breathing.

What might be slightly less well understood regarding the sign of the Twins is that you are a natural listener too. One of the reasons for your popularity is that you always seem interested in what those around you have to say. And beneath this desire to know is a latent ability to understand so much about your friends and relatives at an almost instinctive level. Gemini individuals can keep moving forward, even against heavy odds, just as long as a particular project or task feels right, and you should never underestimate the power of your instincts.

The level of your energy, and the way you project it into everything you do, can be inclined to leave others breathless. This is one of your secrets of success because you can be at the winning post so often, whilst others are still putting on their shoes. You are not a trend follower but rather a trendsetter, and no matter if you are on the dance floor of a trendy club, or on a senior citizens' trip to the coast, you are likely to be the centre of attention. The enterprising, interesting Gemini individual skips through life like a barefoot child and elicits just as much joy from those who stand and watch.

Beneath the happy-go-lucky exterior is a great deal more savvy than many astrologers were once willing to grant to the sign of the Twins. However, the advent of the multimedia age has brought Gemini to a society that it not only understands, but in which it excels. On the telephone, the computer and especially the World Wide Web, you spread your sense of fun and offer everyone you meet an invigorating dose of your enthusiasm, knowledge and zest for life.

Beneath the surface

It is likely that most Gemini individuals would consider themselves to be uncomplicated and easy to understand. 'What you see is what you get' seems to be a statement made extremely often by those born under this zodiac sign. It isn't at all true. On the contrary, the Gemini nature is multi faceted, cranky and often obscure. In short, you have more skins than a Spanish onion. If Geminis have often been referred to as 'superficial' or 'shallow' they probably only have themselves to blame, since they are the first to describe themselves this way. But the truth is that you are a deep thinker – in fact one of the deepest of all. The only reason you don't consider yourself in this light is that your thought processes, like your speech, are lightning fast.

Because of its chatterbox ways, Gemini is often a very misunderstood zodiac sign. But listen to yourself talking. Many of the statements you make to those around you will be ended in questions such as 'Don't you think?'. Why should this be so? Well the fact is that you are never so certain of yourself as you want to give the impression of being, and as a result you invariably seek the confirmation of the world at large that your ideas and plans are sound. If the response you want is late, or not forthcoming at all, you tend to feel insecure and start to fidget. In time this leads to worrying, the worst possible state for the Gemini mind. The dividing line between mental and physical is not at all well defined in your case, so you will often seem most fatigued at those times when you are less than sure of your direction in life.

You almost always start out with the right intentions and would never deliberately hurt another individual. To your very core you are generous and kind. Unfortunately in a busy schedule there isn't always time to let your sensitivity show, and especially not when you live your life constantly in the fast lane. It is almost instinctive for Geminis to divide their lives into 'the job I am doing now', 'the task I will be undertaking in a few minutes' and 'the things I am planning for later'. But even your mind is only capable of so much, so it's essential that you find moments to stop the whirl and buzz of your innermost thoughts. To do so is the hardest task you will undertake, but it's the surest path to health and success that you can ever choose.

Making the best of yourself

It is quite clear that you were never cut out to be a monk or a nun, or at least not of the contemplative sort. Mental desert islands are a natural torture chamber to your zodiac sign and so it's obvious, right from the start, that you need other people just as much as plants need rain. On the other hand, you also need to stop thinking that you can be in control of everything. The hardest lesson for any Gemini to learn is to be selective. Gemini sees life like a wonderfully prepared buffet at which every successive dish offers something absolutely delicious. The idea of trying some of the treats later simply doesn't occur and at the level of daily life the result can often be mental indigestion. Concentration is the key, though without losing the essential freshness and appeal that is the hallmark of your natural personality. 'One job at once' is the best adage, but it doesn't come easy for you.

Your natural talents are suited to intellectual browsing, so you are definitely at your best where flexibility is present. The chances are that you don't really enjoy getting your hands dirty, but even this doesn't really matter as long as you are learning something on the way. You revel in absorbing responsibility and tend to think on your feet. Travel is important to you, not only because it broadens your mind, but also because you are naturally good at languages. You possess a very human touch; you are not frightened to show your emotions and work well alongside others. However, you might function even better if you maintained confidence in your decisions and tried rather less than you sometimes do to be popular with everyone. This comes easier when you are dealing with subject matter that you understand fully, and that in turn takes concentration, which you can only cultivate with practice.

The impressions you give

This section may appeal the most to Gemini subjects because you care deeply about the opinions others have of you. To a certain extent everything you do in a public sense is a sort of performance and just like an actor, you are interested in what the critics have to say. To a great extent you can relax, because there's a good chance that you are much loved. How could it be otherwise? You spread sunshine wherever you go, though it has to be said that you can promote a good deal of confusion too on occasions.

You have to be prepared to take on board the fact that some people will like you more than others do. This is a natural consequence of being such an upfront person. There are people who swim around in the sea of life without making so much as a ripple, but you are definitely not one of them. Some of the individuals you meet will simply not be turned on by the gregarious, enthusiastic, go-getting creature that you are. Once you understand this fact, and stop trying to force your attentions in the wrong direction, your life will be happier as a result.

Another way that you can help yourself is to cultivate humility. Gemini people know at least something about almost everything but there is truth in the adage that 'a little knowledge can be a dangerous thing'. The most successful of those born under the sign of the Twins have learned to defer to experts, most of whom don't take kindly to criticism. You can still maintain your own opinions, but a quiet self-assurance will win you more friends than forcing half-formed opinions on the world at large. On the whole though, you can relax because you are almost certainly more popular than you think you are.

The way forward

Age matters less to Gemini than it does to any other zodiac sign. The fact is that you are always young in your head, no matter how much some of your joints might creak. But even in a physical sense it is important to look after yourself and to recognise those areas that need the most attention. Gemini rules the chest, and especially the lungs, so you should

THE ESSENCE OF GEMINI

ever be a smoker. The sign is also related to the general nervous system, which is almost always pushed to the edge in your frantic attempts to get just as much out of life as possible. Relaxation is just as important as physical exercise, and since you naturally love words, reading is as good as anything. All the same, you shouldn't be constantly trying to learn something, and need to understand that entertainment for its own sake is often enough.

No matter how much your mind wanders, you need to be master of at least one subject – this is the way to success in a professional sense. Whatever your job (and Gemini people are rarely out of work) you will nearly always find yourself in charge of others. Use all the natural understanding that lies at the centre of your being to understand how others tick and you are almost certain to prosper.

On the way through life, professional or social, you can't avoid dealing in gossip, because this is an essential part of the way you function. Casual contacts are inevitable, so you may have hundreds of acquaintances but only a few very close personal friends. However, when you do find yourself absolutely on the same wavelength as another individual, it can be the most enlightening experience imaginable. Geminis often find themselves involved in more than one deep, romantic attachment in their lives, though this is far less likely if your partner is also your best friend.

Don't give in to self-doubt, but at the same time avoid like the plague giving the impression that you know everything. Cultivate patience and spend at least a few minutes each day doing absolutely nothing. Overall, balance is essential, and that isn't always easy to achieve when tottering along the tightrope of life. All the same, a Gemini who is at ease with him- or herself excels socially and grows wiser with every passing day.

GEMINI ON THE CUSP

Old Moore is often asked how astrological profiles are altered for tho
people born at either the beginning or the end of a zodiac sign, o
more properly, on the cusps of a sign. In the case of Gemini this would I
on the 22nd of May and for two or three days after, and similarly at tl
end of the sign, probably from the 19th to the 21st of June. In this year
Astral Diaries, once again, Old Moore sets out to explain the differenc
regarding cuspid signs.

The Taurus Cusp – May 22nd to May 25th

It would be fair to suggest that Gemini tends to predominate over almo
any zodiac sign with which it is associated so that the trends of this mo
capricious and gregarious sign tend to show out well at both cusp
Heavily affected by Taurus, however, you are likely to be steadier ar
more willing to take your time over important matters. Staying power
better and the Taurean cusp inspires a quiet confidence on occasions th
seems to contrast sharply with the more chatty qualities of the Twin
Entrenched attitudes are certainly more likely, with a need to prove
point and to seek objectives through determined effort. Taurus here do
little to stem the generally cheerful qualities of Gemini but there is like
to be a more serious side to the nature and a willingness to exhibit tl
sort of patience that is often lacking in the Sun sign of Gemini.

In matters of love, you are more likely than most Geminis to show
high degree of constancy, even if settling on a partner is a longer proce
in your case. You can't be detached from relationships in the way th
the dyed-in-the-wool Gemini can and it's important for you to kno
that you are loved. Professionally speaking, you have much going for yc
because in addition to the 'get ahead at any cost' quality that comes fro
the direction of the Twins, you are persevering, honourable, steadfa
and reliable. It is probably in matters of business that the most positi
qualities of this astrological matching are to be seen.

Health matters are also stabilised to a great extent on this cusp, part
because the nature is not half as nervy, and more care is taken to get tl
level of rest and relaxation that is just as important to Gemini. Less rus
and push is evident, though a need for change and diversity probab
won't be eradicated from your basic nature. There is a good chance th
you are something of a home bird, at least most of the time, and fami
matters are often paramount in your mind. Probably the most noticeab
trait is your tendency to be more tidy than the orthodox Gemini – whic
some would say is no bad thing.

The Cancer Cusp – June 19th to June 21st

t could be that the gradual slip from the sign of Gemini to that of Cancer is slightly less well defined than is the case for Taurus and Gemini. However, when working as stereotypes Gemini and Cancer are radically different sorts of signs. Gemini seeks to intellectualise everything, so ts catch phrase is 'I think', while Cancer's is 'I feel'. What we would therefore expect, in this case, is a gradually quieter and less fickle nature as the Sun climbs closer to Cancer. You are likely to show more genuine consideration for other people. Actually this is something of a misnomer because Gemini people are very caring too, it's simply a matter of you showing the tendency more, and you are certainly more tied to home and family than any true Gemini would be. A quiet perseverance typifies your individual nature and you are quite prepared to wait for your objectives to mature, which the Twins are less likely to do. Comfort and security are important to you, though, apparently paradoxically, you are a great traveller and love to see fresh fields and pastures new. Given the opportunity you could even find yourself living in some far, distant land.

In affairs of the heart, you are clearly more steadfast than Gemini and love to be loved. The difference here is that Gemini wants to be liked by everyone, but will quickly move on in cases where this proves to be difficult. You, on the other hand, would take any sort of rebuff as a personal insult and would work hard to reverse the situation. Confidence may not be your middle name, but you are supported by the Gemini ability to bluff your way through when necessary, even if the motivation involved is of a more consistent nature.

You may well be a person who has to rest in order to recharge batteries that sometimes run quite low. Your nervous system may not be all that strong on occasions and this fact could manifest itself in the form of stomach troubles of one sort or another. Common sense counts when t comes to looking after yourself and that's something that the sign of Cancer does possess. Whether you are often truly satisfied with yourself and your own efforts may sometimes be in doubt.

GEMINI AND ITS ASCENDANTS

The nature of every individual on the planet is composed of the ric
variety of zodiac signs and planetary positions that were present at th
time of their birth. Your Sun sign, which in your case is Gemini, is one o
the many factors when it comes to assessing the unique person you ar
Probably the most important consideration, other than your Sun sig
is to establish the zodiac sign that was rising over the eastern horizo
at the time that you were born. This is your Ascending or Rising sig
Most popular astrology fails to take account of the Ascendant, and y
its importance remains with you from the very moment of your birtl
through every day of your life. The Ascendant is evident in the way yo
approach the world, and so, when meeting a person for the first time,
is this astrological influence that you are most likely to notice first. O
Ascending sign essentially represents what we appear to be, while the Su
sign is what we feel inside ourselves.

The Ascendant also has the potential for modifying our overall natur
For example, if you were born at a time of day when Gemini was passin
over the eastern horizon (this would be around the time of dawn) the
you would be classed as a double Gemini. As such, you would typify th
zodiac sign, both internally and in your dealings with others. Howeve
if your Ascendant sign turned out to be a Water sign, such as Pisce
there would be a profound alteration of nature, away from the expecte
qualities of Gemini.

One of the reasons why popular astrology often ignores the Ascendar
is that it has always been rather difficult to establish. Old Moore has foun
a way to make this possible by devising an easy-to-use table, which yo
will find on page 156 of this book. Using this, you can establish you
Ascendant sign at a glance. You will need to know your rough time o
birth, then it is simply a case of following the instructions.

For those readers who have no idea of their time of birth it might b
worth allowing a good friend, or perhaps your partner, to read throug
the section that follows this introduction. Someone who deals with yo
on a regular basis may easily discover your Ascending sign, even thoug
you could have some difficulty establishing it for yourself. A goo
understanding of this component of your nature is essential if you wal
to be aware of that 'other person' who is responsible for the way yo
make contact with the world at large. Your Sun sign, Ascendant sig
and the other pointers in this book will, together, allow you a far bette
understanding of what makes you tick as an individual. Peeling bac
the different layers of your astrological make-up can be an enlightenin
experience, and the Ascendant may represent one of the most importar
layers of all.

Gemini with Gemini Ascendant

ou are one of the most fun-loving characters in the zodiac, with a eat sense of humour and the ability to sell refrigerators to Eskimos. ost people would think that you have nerves of steel and that there is othing that lies beyond the scope of your ready wit and silver tongue. nfortunately it isn't quite as simple as this because you bruise easily, pecially when you discover that someone is not as fond of you as they ight be. Routines get on your nerves and you need as much change d diversity as life will allow. You are the life and soul of any party that going on in your vicinity, and you have the ability to mix business and easure so should get on well as a result.

In love you tend to be rather fickle and the double Gemini is inclined dodge from relationship to relationship in pursuit of something that mains rather difficult to define. There are occasions when your life lacks ability and this can be provided by the right sort of personal attachment, suming you manage to find it eventually. It is clear that you are not the siest person to understand, even though you probably think that you not have a complicated bone in your body. Most important of all, you ave many, many friends, and this will be the case all your life.

Gemini with Cancer Ascendant

any astrologers would say that this is a happy combination because me of the more flighty qualities of Gemini are somewhat modified the steady influence of Cancer the Crab. To all intents and purposes u show the friendly and gregarious qualities of Gemini, but there is thoughtful and even sometimes a serious quality that would not be esent in the double Gemini example above. Looking after people is gh on your list of priorities and you do this most of the time. This is ade possible because you have greater staying power than Gemini is ually said to possess and you can easily see fairly complicated situations rough to their conclusion without becoming bored on the way.

The chances are that you will have many friends and that these people ow great concern for your well-being, because you choose them refully and show them a great deal of consideration. However, you will ill be on the receiving end of gossip on occasions, and need to treat such tuations with a healthy pinch of salt. Like all Geminis, your nervous stem is not as strong as you would wish to believe and family pressures particular can put great strain on you. Activities of all kinds take your ncy and many people with this combination are attracted to sailing or ind surfing.

Gemini with Leo Ascendant

Many Gemini people think about doing great things, whilst those w
enjoy a Leo Ascendant do much more than simply think. You are the tr
intrepid Gemini but you always keep a sense of humour and are especia
good to be around. Bold and quite fearless, you are inclined to go whe
nobody has gone before, no matter if this is into a precarious busine
venture or up a mountain that has not been previously climbed. It
people such as you who first explored the world and you love to kno
what lies around the next corner and over the far hill.

Kind and loving, you are especially loyal to your friends and wou
do almost anything on their behalf. As a result they show the great
concern for you too. However, there are times when the cat walks alo
and you are probably better at being on your own than would often
the case for the typical Gemini subject. In many ways you are fairly se
contained and don't tend to get bored too much unless you are forc
to do the same things time and time again. You have a great sense of fu
can talk to anyone and usually greet the world with a big smile.

Gemini with Virgo Ascendant

A Virgo Ascendant means that you are ruled by Mercury, both throu
your Sun sign and through the sign that was rising at the time of yo
birth. This means that words are your basic tools in life and you use the
to the full. Some writers have this combination because even speaki
to people virtually all the time is not enough. Although you have ma
friends, you are fairly high-minded which means that you can ma
enemies too. The fact is that people either care very much for you, or e
they don't like you at all. This can be difficult for you to come to ter
with because you don't really set out to cause friction – it often simp
attracts itself to you.

Although you love to travel, home is important too. There is a ba
insecurity in your nature that comes about as a result of an overdose
Mercury, which makes you nervy and sometimes far less confident th
anyone would guess. Success in your life may be slower arriving with th
combination because you are determined to achieve your objectives
your own terms and this can take time. Always a contradiction, often
puzzle to others, your ultimate happiness in life is directly proportional
the effort you put in, though this should not mean wearing yourself o
on the way.

Gemini with Libra Ascendant

What a happy-go-lucky soul you are, and how popular you tend to be with those around you. Libra is, like Gemini, an Air sign and this means that you are the communicator par excellence, even by Gemini standards. It can sometimes be difficult for you to make up your mind about things because Libra does not exactly aid this process, and especially not when it is allied to Mercurial Gemini. Frequent periods of deep thought are necessary and meditation would do you a great deal of good. All the same, although you might sometimes be rather unsure of yourself, you are rarely without a certain balance. Clean and tidy surroundings suit you the best, though this is far from easy to achieve because you are invariably dashing off to some place or other, so you really need someone to sort things out in your absence.

The most important fact of all is that you are much loved by your friends, of which there are likely to be very many. Because you are so willing to help them out, in return they are usually there when it matters and they would probably go to almost any length on your behalf. You exhibit a fine sense of justice and will usually back those in trouble. Charities tend to be attractive to you and you do much on behalf of those who live on the fringes of society or people who are truly alone.

Gemini with Scorpio Ascendant

What you are and what you appear to be can be two entirely different things with this combination. Although you appear to be every bit as chatty and even as flighty as Gemini tends to be, nothing could be further from the truth. In reality you have many deep and penetrating insights, all of which are geared towards sorting out potential problems before they come along. Few people would have the ability to pull the wool over your eyes and you show a much more astute face to the world than is often the case for Gemini taken on its own. The level of your confidence, although not earth-shattering, is much greater with this combination, and you would not be thwarted once you had made up your mind.

There is a slight danger here however because Gemini is always inclined to nerve problems of one sort or another. In the main these are light and fleeting, though the presence of Scorpio can intensify reactions and heighten the possibility of depression, which would not be at all fortunate. The best way round this potential problem is to have a wealth of friends, plenty to do and the sort of variety in your life that suits your Mercury ruler. Financial success is not too difficult to achieve with this combination, mainly because you can easily earn money and then have a natural ability to hold on to it.

Gemini with Sagittarius Ascendant

'Tomorrow is another day!' This is your belief and you stick to it. Ther isn't a brighter or more optimistic soul to be found than you and almos everyone you come into contact with is touched by the fact. Dashin about from one place to another, you manage to get more things don in one day than most other people would achieve in a week. Of cours this explains why you are so likely to wear yourself out, and it means tha frequent periods of absolute rest are necessary if you are to remain trul healthy and happy. Sagittarius makes you brave and sometimes a littl headstrong, so you need to curb your natural enthusiasms now and agair whilst you stop to think about the consequences of some of your action

It's not really certain if you do 'think' in the accepted sense of th word, because the lightning qualities of both these signs mean that you reactions are second to none. However, you are not indestructible an you put far more pressure on yourself than would often be sensibl Routines are not your thing at all and many of you manage to hold dow two or more jobs at once. It might be an idea to stop and smell th flowers on the way and you could certainly do with putting your feet u much more than you do. However, you probably won't even have rea this far into the passage because you will almost certainly have somethin far more important to do!

Gemini with Capricorn Ascendant

A much more careful and considered combination is evident here. Yo still have the friendly and chatty qualities of Gemini, though you als possess an astute, clever and deep-thinking quality which can really ad bite to the Mercurial aspects of your nature. Although you rarely seer to take yourself or anyone else all that seriously, in reality you are n easily fooled and usually know the direction in which you are headin The practical application of your thought processes matter to you an you always give of your best, especially in any professional situatio This combination provides the very best business mind that any Gemir could have and, unlike other versions of the sign, you are willing to allo matters to mature. This quality cannot be overstated, and leads to a for of ultimate achievement that many other Geminis would only guess at.

Family matters are important to you and your home is a special plac of retreat, even though you are also willing to get out and meet the worl which is the prerogative of all Gemini types. There are times when yo genuinely wish to remain quiet, and when such times arise you may nee to explain the situation to some of the bemused people surrounding yo Above all you look towards material gain, though without ever losin your sense of humour.

Gemini with Aquarius Ascendant

you were around in the 1960s there is every chance that you were the first to go around with flowers in your hair. You are unconventional, original, quirky and entertaining. Few people would fail to notice your presence and you take life as it comes, even though on most occasions you are firmly in the driving seat. In all probability you care very much about the planet on which you live and the people with whom you share . Not everyone understands you, but that does not really matter, for you have more than enough communication skills to put your message across intact. You should avoid wearing yourself out by worrying about things that you cannot control and you definitely gain from taking time out to meditate. However, whether or not you allow yourself that luxury remains to be seen.

If you are not the most communicative form of Gemini subject then you must come a close second. Despite this fact, much of what you have to say makes real sense and you revel in the company of interesting, intelligent and stimulating people, whose opinions on a host of matters will add to your own considerations. You are a true original in every sense of the word and the mere fact of your presence in the world is bound to add to the enjoyment of life experienced by the many people with whom you make contact in your daily life.

Gemini with Pisces Ascendant

There is great duality inherent with this combination, and sometimes this can cause a few problems. Part of the trouble stems from the fact that you often fail to realise what you want from life and you could also be accused of failing to take the time out to think things through carefully enough. You are reactive, and although you have every bit of the natural charm that typifies the sign of Gemini, you are more prone to periods of self-doubt and confusion. However, you should not allow these facts to get you down too much because you are also genuinely loved and have a tremendous capacity to look after others, a factor which is more important to you than any other. It's true that personal relationships can sometimes be a cause of difficulty for you, partly because your constant need to know what makes other people tick could drive them up the wall. Accepting people at face value seems to be the best key to happiness of a personal sort and there are occasions when your very real and natural intuition has to be put on hold.

It's likely that you are an original, particularly in the way you dress. An early rebellious stage often gives way to a more comfortable form of eccentricity. When you are at your best just about everyone adores you.

Gemini with Aries Ascendant

A fairly jolly combination this, though by no means easy for others
come to terms with. You fly about from pillar to post and rarely st
long enough to take a breath. Admittedly this suits your own needs ve
well, but it can be a source of some disquiet to those around you, sin
they may not possess your energy or motivation. Those who know y
well are deeply in awe of your capacity to keep going long after almo
everyone else would have given up and gone home, though this qual
is not always wonderful, because it means that you put more pressure (
your nervous system than just about any other astrological combinatio

You need to be mindful of your nervous system, which responds
the erratic, Mercurial quality of Gemini. Problems only really arise wh
the Aries part of you makes demands that the Gemini component fin
difficult to deal with. There are paradoxes galore here and some of the
need sorting out if you are ever fully to understand yourself, or are to
in a position when others know what makes you tick.

In relationships you might be a little fickle, but you are a veritab
charmer and never stuck for the right words, no matter who you a
dealing with. Your tenacity knows no bounds, though perhaps it shoul

Gemini with Taurus Ascendant

This is a generally happy combination which finds you better able
externalise the cultured and creative qualities that are inherent in yo
Taurean side. You love to be around interesting and stimulating peop
and tend to be just as talkative as the typical Gemini is expected to be. T
reason why Gemini helps here is because it lightens the load somewh
Taurus is not the most introspective sign of the zodiac, but it does ha
some of that quality, and a Gemini Sun allows you to speak your min
more freely and, as a result, to know yourself better too.

Although your mind tends to be fairly logical, you also enjoy flash
of insight that can cause you to behave in a less rational way from tin
to time. This is probably no bad thing because life will never be borin
with you around. You try to convince yourself that you take on board
the many and varied opinions that come back at you from others, thoug
there is a slight danger of intellectual snobbery if the responses you g
are not the expected ones. You particularly like clean houses, funny peop
and probably fast cars. Financial rewards can come thick and fast to t
Taurus-Ascendant Gemini when the logical but still inspirational mind
firmly harnessed to practical matters.

HE MOON AND THE PART IT PLAYS IN YOUR LIFE

n astrology the Moon is probably the single most important heavenly body after the Sun. Its unique position, as partner to the Earth on its urney around the solar system, means that the Moon appears to pass ough the signs of the zodiac extremely quickly. The zodiac position of e Moon at the time of your birth plays a great part in personal character d is especially significant in the build-up of your emotional nature.

Sun Moon Cycles

e first lunar cycle deals with the part the position of the Moon plays ative to your Sun sign. I have made the fluctuations of this pattern easy you to understand by means of a simple cyclic graph. It appears on e first page of each 'Your Month At A Glance', under the title 'Highs d Lows'. The graph displays the lunar cycle and you will soon learn to derstand how its movements have a bearing on your level of energy d your abilities.

Your Own Moon Sign

scovering the position of the Moon at the time of your birth has always en notoriously difficult because tracking the complex zodiac positions the Moon is not easy. This process has been reduced to three simple ges with Old Moore's unique Lunar Tables. A breakdown of the oon's zodiac positions can be found from page 25 onwards, so that ce you know what your Moon Sign is, you can see what part this plays the overall build-up of your personal character.

If you follow the instructions on the next page you will soon be able work out exactly what zodiac sign the Moon occupied on the day that u were born and you can then go on to compare the reading for this sition with those of your Sun sign and your Ascendant. It is partly the mparison between these three important positions that goes towards aking you the unique individual you are.

HOW TO DISCOVER YOUR MOON SIGN

This is a three-stage process. You may need a pen and a piece of pa
but if you follow the instructions below the process should only tak
minute or so.

STAGE 1 First of all you need to know the Moon Age at the time
your birth. If you look at Moon Table 1, on page 21, you will find all
years between 1916 and 2014 down the left side. Find the year of y
birth and then trace across to the right to the month of your birth. Wh
the two intersect you will find a number. This is the date of the N
Moon in the month that you were born. You now need to count forw
the number of days between the New Moon and your own birthd
For example, if the New Moon in the month of your birth was sho
as being the 6th and you were born on the 20th, your Moon Age I
would be 14. If the New Moon in the month of your birth came at
your birthday, you need to count forward from the New Moon in
previous month. Whatever the result, jot this number down so that y
do not forget it.

STAGE 2 Take a look at Moon Table 2 on page 22. Down the left ha
column look for the date of your birth. Now trace across to the mor
of your birth. Where the two meet you will find a letter. Copy this let
down alongside your Moon Age Day.

STAGE 3 Moon Table 3 on page 22 will supply you with the zodiac s
the Moon occupied on the day of your birth. Look for your Moon A
Day down the left hand column and then for the letter you found in St
2. Where the two converge you will find a zodiac sign and this is the s
occupied by the Moon on the day that you were born.

Your Zodiac Moon Sign Explained

You will find a profile of all zodiac Moon Signs on pages 23 to 26, show
in yet another way how astrology helps to make you into the individ
that you are. In each daily entry of the Astral Diary you can find
zodiac position of the Moon for every day of the year. This also allo
you to discover your lunar birthdays. Since the Moon passes throu
all the signs of the zodiac in about a month, you can expect someth
like twelve lunar birthdays each year. At these times you are likely to
emotionally steady and able to make the sort of decisions that have r
lasting value.

MOON TABLE 1

AR	APR	MAY	JUN	YEAR	APR	MAY	JUN	YEAR	APR	MAY	JUN
)16	3	2	1/30	1949	28	27	26	1982	23	21	20
)17	22	20	19	1950	17	17	15	1983	13	12	11
)18	11	10	8	1951	6	6	4	1984	1	1/30	29
)19	30	29	27	1952	24	23	22	1985	20	19	18
)20	18	18	16	1953	13	13	11	1986	9	8	7
)21	8	7	6	1954	3	2	1/30	1987	28	27	26
)22	27	26	25	1955	22	21	20	1988	16	15	14
)23	16	15	14	1956	11	10	8	1989	6	5	3
)24	4	3	2	1957	29	29	27	1990	25	24	22
)25	23	22	21	1958	19	18	17	1991	13	13	11
)26	12	11	10	1959	8	7	6	1992	3	2	1/30
)27	2	1/30	29	1960	26	26	24	1993	22	21	20
)28	20	19	18	1961	15	14	13	1994	11	10	9
)29	9	9	7	1962	5	4	2	1995	30	29	27
)30	28	28	26	1963	23	23	21	1996	18	18	17
)31	18	17	16	1964	12	11	10	1997	7	6	5
)32	6	5	4	1965	1	1/30	29	1998	26	25	24
)33	24	24	23	1966	20	19	18	1999	16	15	13
)34	13	13	12	1967	9	8	7	2000	4	4	2
)35	3	2	1/30	1968	28	27	26	2001	23	23	21
)36	21	20	19	1969	16	15	14	2002	12	12	10
)37	12	10	8	1970	6	6	4	2003	1	1/30	29
)38	30	29	27	1971	25	24	22	2004	18	16	15
)39	19	19	17	1972	13	13	11	2005	8	8	6
)40	7	7	6	1973	3	2	1/30	2006	27	27	26
)41	26	26	24	1974	22	21	20	2007	17	17	15
)42	15	15	13	1975	11	11	9	2008	6	5	4
)43	4	4	2	1976	29	29	27	2009	26	25	23
)44	22	22	20	1977	18	18	16	2010	14	14	12
)45	12	11	10	1978	7	7	5	2011	3	3	2
)46	2	1/30	29	1979	26	26	24	2012	21	20	19
)47	20	19	18	1980	15	14	13	2013	10	10	8
)48	9	9	7	1981	4	4	2	2014	30	29	27

TABLE 2

DAY	MAY	JUN
1	M	O
2	M	P
3	M	P
4	M	P
5	M	P
6	M	P
7	M	P
8	M	P
9	M	P
10	M	P
11	M	P
12	N	Q
13	N	Q
14	N	Q
15	N	Q
16	N	Q
17	N	Q
18	N	Q
19	N	Q
20	N	Q
21	N	Q
22	O	R
23	O	R
24	O	R
25	O	R
26	O	R
27	O	R
28	O	R
29	O	R
30	O	R
31	O	–

TABLE 3

M/D	M	N	O	P	Q	R	S
0	TA	GE	GE	GE	CA	CA	CA
1	GE	GE	GE	CA	CA	CA	LE
2	GE	GE	CA	CA	CA	LE	LE
3	GE	CA	CA	CA	LE	LE	LE
4	CA	CA	CA	LE	LE	LE	VI
5	CA	LE	LE	LE	VI	VI	VI
6	LE	LE	LE	VI	VI	VI	LI
7	LE	LE	VI	VI	VI	LI	LI
8	LE	VI	VI	VI	LI	LI	LI
9	VI	VI	VI	LI	LI	SC	SC
10	VI	LI	LI	LI	SC	SC	SC
11	LI	LI	SC	SC	SC	SA	SA
12	LI	LI	SC	SC	SA	SA	SA
13	LI	SC	SC	SC	SA	SA	SA
14	LI	SC	SC	SA	SA	SA	CP
15	SC	SA	SA	SA	CP	CP	CP
16	SC	SA	SA	CP	CP	CP	AQ
17	SA	SA	CP	CP	CP	AQ	AQ
18	SA	CP	CP	CP	AQ	AQ	AQ
19	SA	CP	CP	AQ	AQ	AQ	PI
20	CP	AQ	AQ	AQ	PI	PI	PI
21	CP	AQ	AQ	PI	PI	PI	AR
22	AQ	AQ	PI	PI	PI	AR	AR
23	AQ	PI	PI	PI	AR	AR	AR
24	AQ	PI	PI	AR	AR	AR	TA
25	PI	AR	AR	AR	TA	TA	TA
26	PI	AR	AR	TA	TA	TA	GE
27	AR	AR	TA	TA	TA	GE	GE
28	AR	TA	TA	TA	GE	GE	GE
29	AR	TA	TA	GE	GE	GE	CA

AR = Aries, TA = Taurus, GE = Gemini, CA = Cancer, LE = Leo, VI = Virgo, LI = Lib
SC = Scorpio, SA = Sagittarius, CP = Capricorn, AQ = Aquarius, PI = Pisces

MOON SIGNS

Moon in Aries

u have a strong imagination, courage, determination and a desire to do
ngs in your own way and forge your own path through life.

Originality is a key attribute; you are seldom stuck for ideas although
ur mind is changeable and you could take the time to focus on individual
ks. Often quick-tempered, you take orders from few people and live life
a fast pace. Avoid health problems by taking regular time out for rest
d relaxation.

Emotionally, it is important that you talk to those you are closest to
d work out your true feelings. Once you discover that people are there
help, there is less necessity for you to do everything yourself.

Moon in Taurus

e Moon in Taurus gives you a courteous and friendly manner, which
ans you are likely to have many friends.

The good things in life mean a lot to you, as Taurus is an Earth
n that delights in experiences which please the senses. Hence you are
obably a lover of good food and drink, which may in turn mean you
ed to keep an eye on the bathroom scales, especially as looking good is
o important to you.

Emotionally you are fairly stable and you stick by your own standards.
ureans do not respond well to change. Intuition also plays an important
rt in your life.

Moon in Gemini

u have a warm-hearted character, sympathetic and eager to help others.
times reserved, you can also be articulate and chatty: this is part of the
radox of Gemini, which always brings duplicity to the nature. You are
terested in current affairs, have a good intellect, and are good company
d likely to have many friends. Most of your friends have a high opinion
you and would be ready to defend you should the need arise. However,
is is usually unnecessary, as you are quite capable of defending yourself
any verbal confrontation.

Travel is important to your inquisitive mind and you find intellectual
mulus in mixing with people from different cultures. You also gain
uch from reading, writing and the arts but you do need plenty of rest
d relaxation in order to avoid fatigue.

Moon in Cancer

The Moon in Cancer at the time of birth is a fortunate position as Canc
is the Moon's natural home. This means that the qualities of compassic
and understanding given by the Moon are especially enhanced in yo
nature, and you are friendly and sociable and cope well with emotior
pressures. You cherish home and family life, and happily do the domest
tasks. Your surroundings are important to you and you hate squalor ar
filth. You are likely to have a love of music and poetry.

Your basic character, although at times changeable like the Moon itse
depends on symmetry. You aim to make your surroundings comfortat
and harmonious, for yourself and those close to you.

Moon in Leo

The best qualities of the Moon and Leo come together to make yo
warmhearted, fair, ambitious and self-confident. With good organisation
abilities, you invariably rise to a position of responsibility in your chose
career. This is fortunate as you don't enjoy being an 'also-ran' and wou
rather be an important part of a small organisation than a menial in
large one.

You should be lucky in love, and happy, provided you put in the effc
to make a comfortable home for yourself and those close to you. It
likely that you will have a love of pleasure, sport, music and literatur
Life brings you many rewards, most of them as a direct result of your ov
efforts, although you may be luckier than average and ready to make th
best of any situation.

Moon in Virgo

You are endowed with good mental abilities and a keen recepti
memory, but you are never ostentatious or pretentious. Naturally qui
reserved, you still have many friends, especially of the opposite se
Marital relationships must be discussed carefully and worked at so th
they remain harmonious, as personal attachments can be a problem if yc
do not give them your full attention.

Talented and persevering, you possess artistic qualities and are
good homemaker. Earning your honours through genuine merit, yc
work long and hard towards your objectives but show little pride in yo
achievements. Many short journeys will be undertaken in your life.

Moon in Libra

With the Moon in Libra you are naturally popular and make friends easily. People like you, probably more than you realise, you bring fun to a party and are a natural diplomat. For all its good points, Libra is not the most stable of astrological signs and, as a result, your emotions can be a little unstable too. Therefore, although the Moon in Libra is said to be good for love and marriage, your Sun sign and Rising sign will have an important effect on your emotional and loving qualities.

You must remember to relate to others in your decision-making. Co-operation is crucial because Libra represents the 'balance' of life that can only be achieved through harmonious relationships. Conformity is not easy for you because Libra, an Air sign, likes its independence.

Moon in Scorpio

Some people might call you pushy. In fact, all you really want to do is to live life to the full and protect yourself and your family from the pressures of life. Take care to avoid giving the impression of being sarcastic or impulsive and use your energies wisely and constructively.

You have great courage and you invariably achieve your goals by force of personality and sheer effort. You are fond of mystery and are good at predicting the outcome of situations and events. Travel experiences can be beneficial to you.

You may experience problems if you do not take time to examine your motives in a relationship, and also if you allow jealousy, always a feature of Scorpio, to cloud your judgement.

Moon in Sagittarius

The Moon in Sagittarius helps to make you a generous individual with humanitarian qualities and a kind heart. Restlessness may be intrinsic as your mind is seldom still. Perhaps because of this, you have a need for change that could lead you to several major moves during your adult life. You are not afraid to stand your ground when you know your judgement is right, you speak directly and have good intuition.

At work you are quick, efficient and versatile and so you make an ideal employee. You need work to be intellectually demanding and do not enjoy tedious routines.

In relationships, you anger quickly if faced with stupidity or deception, though you are just as quick to forgive and forget. Emotionally, there are times when your heart rules your head.

Moon in Capricorn

The Moon in Capricorn makes you popular and likely to come into the public eye in some way. The watery Moon is not entirely comfortable in the Earth sign of Capricorn and this may lead to some difficulties in the early years of life. An initial lack of creative ability and indecision must be overcome before the true qualities of patience and perseverance inherent in Capricorn can show through.

You have good administrative ability and are a capable worker, and if you are careful you can accumulate wealth. But you must be cautious and take professional advice in partnerships, as you are open to deception. You may be interested in social or welfare work, which suit your organisational skills and sympathy for others.

Moon in Aquarius

The Moon in Aquarius makes you an active and agreeable person with a friendly, easy-going nature. Sympathetic to the needs of others, you flourish in a laid-back atmosphere. You are broad-minded, fair and open to suggestion, although sometimes you have an unconventional quality which others can find hard to understand.

You are interested in the strange and curious, and in old articles and places. You enjoy trips to these places and gain much from them. Political, scientific and educational work interests you and you might choose a career in science or technology.

Money-wise, you make gains through innovation and concentration and Lunar Aquarians often tackle more than one job at a time. In love you are kind and honest.

Moon in Pisces

You have a kind, sympathetic nature, somewhat retiring at times, but you always take account of others' feelings and help when you can.

Personal relationships may be problematic, but as life goes on you can learn from your experiences and develop a better understanding of yourself and the world around you.

You have a fondness for travel, appreciate beauty and harmony and hate disorder and strife. You may be fond of literature and would make a good writer or speaker yourself. You have a creative imagination and may come across as an incurable romantic. You have strong intuition, maybe bordering on a mediumistic quality, which sets you apart from the mass. You may not be rich in cash terms, but your personal gifts are worth more than gold.

GEMINI IN LOVE

iscover how compatible you are with people from the same and other gns of the zodiac. Five stars equals a match made in heaven!

Gemini meets Gemini

enerally speaking, this match can be very successful because although emini people can be insecure, they basically feel they are quite 'together' rts of people. Consequently, they experience a meeting of minds with llow Twins. This relationship won't work at a distance, and depends a degree of intimacy to negate the more flighty and showy qualities f the sign. Infidelity could be a potential problem, especially with two emini people in the picture, but jealousy doesn't usually prevail. Star ting: ****

Gemini meets Cancer

his is often a very good match. Cancer is a very caring sign and quite daptable. Geminis are untidy, have butterfly minds and are usually full f a thousand different schemes which Cancerians take in their stride d even relish. They can often be the 'wind beneath the wings' of their emini partners. In return, Gemini can eradicate some of the Cancerian notional insecurity and is more likely to be faithful in thought, word d deed to Cancer than to almost any other sign. Star rating: ****

Gemini meets Leo

here can be problems here, but Gemini is adaptable enough to overcome any of them. Leo is a go-getter and might sometimes rail against emini's flighty tendencies, while Gemini's mental disorganisation n undermine Leo's practicality. However, Leo is cheerful and enjoys emini's jokey, flippant qualities. At times of personal intimacy, the two gns should be compatible. Leo and Gemini share very high ideals, but eo will stick at them for longer. Patience is needed on both sides for the lationship to develop. Star rating: ***

Gemini meets Virgo

he fact that both these signs are ruled by the planet Mercury might first seem good but, unfortunately, Mercury works very differently each of them. Gemini is untidy, flighty, quick, changeable and easily ored, while Virgo is fastidious, steady and constant. If Virgo is willing accept some anarchy, all can be well, but this not usually the case. irgoans are deep thinkers and may find Gemini a little superficial. This air can be compatible intellectually, though even this side isn't without problems. Star rating: ***

Gemini meets Libra

One of the best possible zodiac combinations. Libra and Gemini are both Air signs, which leads to a meeting of minds. Both signs simply love to have a good time, although Libra is the tidiest and less forgetful. Gemini's capricious nature won't bother Libra, who acts as a stabilising influence. Life should generally run smoothly, and any rows are likely to be short and sharp. Both parties genuinely like each other, which is of paramount importance in a relationship and, ultimately, there isn't a better reason for being or staying together. Star rating: *****

Gemini meets Scorpio

There could be problems here. Scorpio is one of the deepest and least understood of all the zodiac signs, which at first seems like a challenge to intellectual Gemini, who thinks it can solve anything. But the deeper the Gemini digs, the further down Scorpio goes. Meanwhile, Scorpio may be finding Gemini thoughtless, shallow and even downright annoying. Gemini is often afraid of Scorpio's strength, and the sting in its tail, both of which the perceptive Twins can instinctively recognise. Anything is possible, but the outlook for this match is less than promising. Star rating: **

Gemini meets Sagittarius

A paradoxical relationship this. On paper, the two signs have much in common, but unfortunately, they are often so alike that life turns into a fiercely fought competition. Both signs love change and diversity and both want to be the life and soul of the party. But in life there must always be a leader and a follower, and neither of this pair wants to be second. Both also share a tendency towards infidelity, which may develop into a problem as time passes. This could be an interesting match, but not necessarily successful. Star rating: **

Gemini meets Capricorn

Gemini has a natural fondness for Capricorn, which at first may be mutual. However, Capricorn is very organised, practical and persevering, and always achieves its goals in the end. Gemini starts out like this, but then changes direction on the way, using a more instinctive and evolutionary approach than the Goat that may interfere with the progress of mutual objectives. To compensate, Gemini helps Capricorn to avoid taking itself too seriously, while Capricorn brings a degree of stability into Gemini's world. When this pairing does work, though, it will be spectacular! Star rating: ***

Gemini meets Aquarius

Aquarius is commonly mistaken for a Water sign, but in fact it's ruled by the Air element, and this is the key to its compatibility with Gemini. Both signs mix freely socially, and each has an insatiable curiosity. There's plenty of action, lots of love but very little rest, and so great potential for success if they don't wear each other out! Aquarius revels in its own eccentricity, and encourages Gemini to emulate this. Theirs will be an unconventional household, but almost everyone warms to this crazy and unpredictable couple. Star rating: *****

Gemini meets Pisces

Gemini likes to think of itself as intuitive and intellectual, and indeed sometimes it is, but it will never understand Pisces' dark depths. Another stumbling block is that both Gemini and Pisces are 'split' signs – the twins and the two Fishes – which means that both are capable of dual personalities. There won't be any shortage of affection, but the real question has to be how much these people ultimately feel they have in common. Pisces is extremely kind, and so is Gemini most of the time. But Pisces does altogether too much soul-searching for Gemini, who might eventually become bored. Star rating: ***

Gemini meets Aries

Don't expect peace and harmony with this combination, although what comes along instead might make up for any disagreements. Gemini has a very fertile imagination, while Aries has the tenacity to make reality from fantasy. Combined, they have a sizzling relationship. There are times when it seems as though both parties will explode with indignation and something has to give. But even if there are clashes, making them up will always be most enjoyable! Mutual financial success is very likely in this match. Star rating: ****

Gemini meets Taurus

Gemini people can really infuriate the generally steady Taurean nature as they are so untidy, which is a complete reversal of the Taurean ethos. At first this won't matter; Mr or Miss Gemini is enchanting, entertaining and very different. But time will tell, and that's why this potential relationship only has two stars. There is some hope, however, because Taurus can curb some of the excesses of the Twins, whilst Gemini is more than capable of preventing the Bull from taking itself too seriously. Star rating: **

VENUS:
THE PLANET OF LOVE

If you look up at the sky around sunset or sunrise you will often se
Venus in close attendance to the Sun. It is arguably one of the mo
beautiful sights of all and there is little wonder that historically it becam
associated with the goddess of love. But although Venus does play a
important part in the way you view love and in the way others see yo
romantically, this is only one of the spheres of influence that it enjoys i
your overall character.

Venus has a part to play in the more cultured side of your life and h
much to do with your appreciation of art, literature, music and gener
creativity. Even the way you look is responsive to the part of the zodia
that Venus occupied at the start of your life, though this fact is also dow
to your Sun sign and Ascending sign. If, at the time you were born, Venu
occupied one of the more gregarious zodiac signs, you will be more like
to wear your heart on your sleeve, as well as to be more attracted t
entertainment, social gatherings and good company. If on the other han
Venus occupied a quiet zodiac sign at the time of your birth, you woul
tend to be more retiring and less willing to shine in public situations.

It's good to know what part the planet Venus plays in your life for
can have a great bearing on the way you appear to the rest of the worl
and since we all have to mix with others, you can learn to make the ve
best of what Venus has to offer you.

One of the great complications in the past has always been trying t
establish exactly what zodiac position Venus enjoyed when you were bor
because the planet is notoriously difficult to track. However, I have solve
that problem by creating a table that is exclusive to your Sun sign, whic
you will find on the following page.

Establishing your Venus sign could not be easier. Just look up the ye
of your birth on the page opposite and you will see a sign of the zodia
This was the sign that Venus occupied in the period covered by your sig
in that year. If Venus occupied more than one sign during the perio
this is indicated by the date on which the sign changed, and the nam
of the new sign. For instance, if you were born in 1950, Venus was i
Gemini until the 8th June, after which time it was in Cancer. If you wer
born before 8th June your Venus sign is Gemini, if you were born on c
after 8th June, your Venus sign is Cancer. Once you have established th
position of Venus at the time of your birth, you can then look in the page
which follow to see how this has a bearing on your life as a whole.

916 CANCER
917 GEMINI / 10.6 CANCER
918 ARIES / 3.6 TAURUS
919 CANCER / 8.6 LEO
920 TAURUS / 3.6 GEMINI
921 ARIES / 3.6 TAURUS
922 GEMINI / 26.5 CANCER /
    21.6 LEO
923 TAURUS / 15.6 GEMINI
924 CANCER
925 GEMINI / 9.6 CANCER
926 ARIES / 2.6 TAURUS
927 CANCER / 8.6 LEO
928 TAURUS / 30.5 GEMINI
929 ARIES / 4.6 TAURUS
930 GEMINI / 22.5 CANCER /
    21.6 LEO
931 TAURUS / 15.6 GEMINI
932 CANCER
933 GEMINI / 9.6 CANCER
934 ARIES / 2.6 TAURUS
935 CANCER / 8.6 LEO
936 TAURUS / 30.5 GEMINI
937 ARIES / 4.6 TAURUS
938 GEMINI / 25.5 CANCER /
    20.6 LEO
939 TAURUS / 14.6 GEMINI
940 CANCER
941 CANCER / 7.6 LEO
942 GEMINI / 8.6 CANCER
943 ARIES / 1.6 TAURUS
944 CANCER / 7.6 LEO
945 TAURUS / 29.5 GEMINI
946 ARIES / 5.6 TAURUS
947 GEMINI / 24.5 CANCER /
    19.6 LEO
948 TAURUS / 14.6 GEMINI
949 CANCER
950 GEMINI / 8.6 CANCER
951 ARIES / 1.6 TAURUS
952 TAURUS / 29.5 GEMINI
953 ARIES / 5.6 TAURUS
954 GEMINI / 24.5 CANCER /
    19.6 LEO
955 TAURUS / 13.6 GEMINI
956 CANCER
957 GEMINI / 7.6 CANCER
958 ARIES / 31.5 TAURUS
959 CANCER / 7.6 LEO
960 TAURUS / 28.5 GEMINI
961 ARIES / 6.6 TAURUS
962 GEMINI / 24.5 CANCER /
    18.6 LEO
963 TAURUS / 13.6 GEMINI
964 CANCER / 17.6 GEMINI
965 GEMINI / 7.6 CANCER
966 ARIES / 31.5 TAURUS

1967 CANCER / 7.6 LEO
1968 TAURUS / 28.5 GEMINI
1969 ARIES / 6.6 TAURUS
1970 GEMINI / 23.5 CANCER /
    18.5 LEO
1971 TAURUS / 12.6 GEMINI
1972 CANCER / 12.6 GEMINI
1973 GEMINI / 6.6 CANCER
1974 ARIES / 30.5 TAURUS
1975 CANCER / 7.6 LEO
1976 TAURUS / 27.5 GEMINI
1977 ARIES / 7.6 TAURUS
1978 GEMINI / 23.5 CANCER /
    17.5 LEO
1979 TAURUS / 12.6 GEMINI
1980 CANCER / 6.6 GEMINI
1981 GEMINI / 6.6 CANCER
1982 ARIES / 30.5 TAURUS
1983 CANCER / 6.6 LEO
1984 TAURUS / 27.5 GEMINI /
    21.6 CANCER
1985 ARIES / 7.6 TAURUS
1986 GEMINI / 22.5 CANCER /
    17.5 LEO
1987 TAURUS / 11.6 GEMINI
1988 CANCER / 27.5 GEMINI
1989 GEMINI / 5.6 CANCER
1990 ARIES / 29.5 TAURUS
1991 CANCER / 6.6 LEO
1992 TAURUS / 26.5 GEMINI /
    20.6 CANCER
1993 ARIES / 7.6 TAURUS
1994 CANCER / 16.6 LEO
1995 TAURUS / 11.6 GEMINI
1996 CANCER / 27.5 GEMINI
1997 GEMINI / 4.6 CANCER
1998 ARIES / 29.5 TAURUS
1999 CANCER / 6.6 LEO
2000 TAURUS / 25.5 GEMINI /
    19.6 CANCER
2001 ARIES / 7.6 TAURUS
2002 CANCER / 15.6 LEO
2003 TAURUS / 11.6 GEMINI
2004 CANCER / 27.5 GEMINI
2005 GEMINI / 2.6 CANCER
2006 ARIES / 29.6 TAURUS
2007 CANCER / 6.6 LEO
2008 TAURUS / 25.5 GEMINI /
    19.6 CANCER
2009 ARIES / 7.6 TAURUS
2010 CANCER / 15.6 LEO
2011 TAURUS / 11.6 GEMINI
2012 CANCER / 27.5 GEMINI
2013 GEMINI / 2.6 CANCER
2014 ARIES / 29.6 TAURUS

31

VENUS THROUGH THE ZODIAC SIGNS

Venus in Aries

Amongst other things, the position of Venus in Aries indicates a fondnes for travel, music and all creative pursuits. Your nature tends to b affectionate and you would try not to create confusion or difficulty fc others if it could be avoided. Many people with this planetary positio have a great love of the theatre, and mental stimulation is of the greate importance. Early romantic attachments are common with Venus in Arie so it is very important to establish a genuine sense of romantic continuit Early marriage is not recommended, especially if it is based on sympath You may give your heart a little too readily on occasions.

Venus in Taurus

You are capable of very deep feelings and your emotions tend to last fc a very long time. This makes you a trusting partner and lover, whos constancy is second to none. In life you are precise and careful and alway try to do things the right way. Although this means an ordered life, whic you are comfortable with, it can also lead you to be rather too fussy fc your own good. Despite your pleasant nature, you are very fixed in you opinions and quite able to speak your mind. Others are attracted to yc and historical astrologers always quoted this position of Venus as bein very fortunate in terms of marriage. However, if you find yourself involve in a failed relationship, it could take you a long time to trust again.

Venus in Gemini

As with all associations related to Gemini, you tend to be quite versatil anxious for change and intelligent in your dealings with the world large. You may gain money from more than one source but you ai equally good at spending it. There is an inference here that you are good communicator, via either the written or the spoken word, and yo love to be in the company of interesting people. Always on the look-ov for culture, you may also be very fond of music, and love to indulg the curious and cultured side of your nature. In romance you tend t have more than one relationship and could find yourself associated wit someone who has previously been a friend or even a distant relative.

Venus in Cancer

ou often stay close to home because you are very fond of family and
njoy many of your most treasured moments when you are with those
ou love. Being naturally sympathetic, you will always do anything you
n to support those around you, even people you hardly know at all.
his charitable side of your nature is your most noticeable trait and is one
' the reasons why others are naturally so fond of you. Being receptive
d in some cases even psychic, you can see through to the soul of most
' those with whom you come into contact. You may not commence too
any romantic attachments but when you do give your heart, it tends to
: unconditionally.

Venus in Leo

must become quickly obvious to almost anyone you meet that you are
nd, sympathetic and yet determined enough to stand up for anyone or
ything that is truly important to you. Bright and sunny, you warm the
orld with your natural enthusiasm and would rarely do anything to hurt
ose around you, or at least not intentionally. In romance you are ardent
d sincere, though some may find your style just a little overpowering.
ains come through your contacts with other people and this could be
pecially true with regard to romance, for love and money often come
nd in hand for those who were born with Venus in Leo. People claim to
derstand you, though you are more complex than you seem.

Venus in Virgo

our nature could well be fairly quiet no matter what your Sun sign might
:, though this fact often manifests itself as an inner peace and would not
event you from being basically sociable. Some delays and even the odd
sappointment in love cannot be ruled out with this planetary position,
ough it's a fact that you will usually find the happiness you look for
 the end. Catapulting yourself into romantic entanglements that you
ow to be rather ill-advised is not sensible, and it would be better to wait
:fore you committed yourself exclusively to any one person. It is the
sence of your nature to serve the world at large and through doing so it
possible that you will attract money at some stage in your life.

Venus in Libra

Venus is very comfortable in Libra and bestows upon those people w'
have this planetary position a particular sort of kindness that is easy
recognise. This is a very good position for all sorts of friendships and a
for romantic attachments that usually bring much joy into your life. F
individuals with Venus in Libra would avoid marriage and since you a
capable of great depths of love, it is likely that you will find a content
personal life. You like to mix with people of integrity and intelligence b
don't take kindly to scruffy surroundings or work that means getting yo
hands too dirty. Careful speculation, good business dealings and mon
through marriage all seem fairly likely.

Venus in Scorpio

You are quite open and tend to spend money quite freely, even on tho
occasions when you don't have very much. Although your intentions a
always good, there are times when you get yourself in to the odd scra
and this can be particularly true when it comes to romance, which y
may come to late or from a rather unexpected direction. Certainly y
have the power to be happy and to make others contented on the w
but you find the odd stumbling block on your journey through life a
it could seem that you have to work harder than those around you. A
result of this, you gain a much deeper understanding of the true value
personal happiness than many people ever do, and are likely to achie
true contentment in the end.

Venus in Sagittarius

You are lighthearted, cheerful and always able to see the funny side of a
situation. These facts enhance your popularity, which is especially hi
with members of the opposite sex. You should never have to look too
to find romantic interest in your life, though it is just possible that y
might be too willing to commit yourself before you are certain that t
person in question is right for you. Part of the problem here extends
other areas of life too. The fact is that you like variety in everything a
so can tire of situations that fail to offer it. All the same, if you choc
wisely and learn to understand your restless side, then great happiness c
be yours.

Venus in Capricorn

The most notable trait that comes from Venus in this position is that it makes you trustworthy and able to take on all sorts of responsibilities in life. People are instinctively fond of you and love you all the more because you are always ready to help those who are in any form of need. Social and business popularity can be yours and there is a magnetic quality to your nature that is particularly attractive in a romantic sense. Anyone who wants a partner for a lover, a spouse and a good friend too would almost certainly look in your direction. Constancy is the hallmark of your nature and unfaithfulness would go right against the grain. You might sometimes be a little too trusting.

Venus in Aquarius

This location of Venus offers a fondness for travel and a desire to try out something new at every possible opportunity. You are extremely easy to get along with and tend to have many friends from varied backgrounds, classes and inclinations. You like to live a distinct sort of life and gain a great deal from moving about, both in a career sense and with regard to your home. It is not out of the question that you could form a romantic attachment to someone who comes from far away or be attracted to a person of a distinctly artistic and original nature. What you cannot stand is jealousy, for you have friends of both sexes and would want to keep things that way.

Venus in Pisces

The first thing people tend to notice about you is your wonderful, warm smile. Being very charitable by nature you will do anything to help others, even if you don't know them well. Much of your life may be spent sorting out situations for other people, but it is very important to feel that you are living for yourself too. In the main, you remain cheerful, and tend to be quite attractive to members of the opposite sex. Where romantic attachments are concerned, you could be drawn to people who are significantly older or younger than yourself or to someone with a unique career or point of view. It might be best for you to avoid marrying whilst you are still very young.

THE ASTRAL DIARY
HOW THE DIAGRAMS WORK

Through the picture diagrams in the Astral Diary I want to help you to plot your year. With them you can see where the positive and negative aspects will be found in each month. To make the most of them, all you have to do is remember where and when!

Let me show you how they work ...

THE MONTH AT A GLANCE

Just as there are twelve separate zodiac signs, so astrologers believe that each sign has twelve separate aspects to life. Each of the twelve segments relates to a different personal aspect. I list them all every month so that their meanings are always clear.

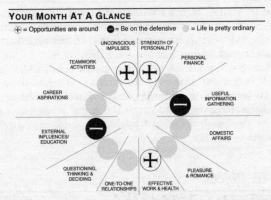

YOUR MONTH AT A GLANCE

⊕ = Opportunities are around ⊖ = Be on the defensive = Life is pretty ordinary

UNCONSCIOUS IMPULSES
STRENGTH OF PERSONALITY
TEAMWORK ACTIVITIES
PERSONAL FINANCE
CAREER ASPIRATIONS
USEFUL INFORMATION GATHERING
EXTERNAL INFLUENCES/ EDUCATION
DOMESTIC AFFAIRS
QUESTIONING, THINKING & DECIDING
PLEASURE & ROMANCE
ONE-TO-ONE RELATIONSHIPS
EFFECTIVE WORK & HEALTH

I have designed this chart to show you how and when these twelve different aspects are being influenced throughout the year. When there is a shaded circle, nothing out of the ordinary is to be expected. However, when a circle turns white with a plus sign, the influence is positive. When the circle is black with a minus sign, it is a negative.

YOUR ENERGY RHYTHM CHART

On the opposite page is a picture diagram in which I link your zodiac group to the rhythm of the Moon. In doing this I have calculated when you will be gaining strength from its influence and equally when you may be weakened by it.

If you think of yourself as being like the tides of the ocean then you may understand how your own energies must also rise and fall. And if you understand how it works and when it is working, then you can better organise your activities to achieve more and get things done more easily.

YOUR ENERGY RHYTHM CHART

At your best on 20th–21st

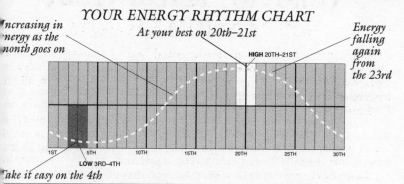

Increasing in energy as the month goes on

HIGH 20TH–21ST

Energy falling again from the 23rd

1ST   5TH   10TH   15TH   20TH   25TH   30TH

LOW 3RD–4TH

Take it easy on the 4th

MOVING PICTURE SCREEN
Love, money, career and vitality measured every week

The diagram at the end of each week is designed to be informative and fun. The arrows move up and down the scale to give you an idea of the strength of your opportunities in each area. If LOVE stands at plus 4, then get out and put yourself about because things are going your way in romance! The further down the arrow goes, the weaker the opportunities. Do note that the diagram is an overall view of your astrological aspects and therefore reflects a trend which may not concur with every day in that cycle.

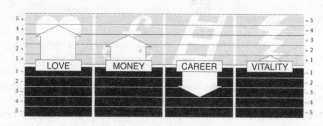

AND FINALLY:

am..

pm..

The two lines that are left blank in each daily entry of the Astral Diary are for your own personal use. You may find them ideal for keeping a check on birthdays or appointments, though it could also be an idea to make notes from the astrological trends and diagrams a few weeks in advance. Some of the lines are marked with a key, which indicates the working of astrological cycles in your life. Look out for them each week as they are the best days to take action or make decisions. The daily text tells you which area of your life to focus on.

= Mercury is retrograde on that day.

GEMINI: YOUR YEAR IN BRIEF

The beginning of the year should prove to be quite interesting for yo and allows you to utilise the very fluid and changeable nature yo possess. Both January and February have their own particular gains an the general speed of life should be increasing as time passes. Not everyon will be following your lead in a professional sense, but that probabl won't bother you too much because during this period you tend to lea by example. Friends should prove to be steadfast.

Be ready to make contact with those you don't see very often durin March and April, and also perhaps to bring one or two new individua into your life. Keep ringing the changes whenever it is possible to do s because, for Gemini, variety genuinely is the spice of life. Romance likely to be high on your agenda during April, at a time when you ai waking up to the possibilities of the spring.

May and June ought to turn out to be the most dynamic part of th year. After all, it is at this time that the Sun visits your part of the zodia and it tends to bring with it a great dose of optimism and some real fla when it comes to new ventures and also travel. By all means give yourse a small pat on the back for something you achieve in May, but ensure th the effort necessary to keep things moving forward is not missing at a during June.

With the arrival of the high summer there isn't much doubt that yo will want to be on the move. This is just as likely in a domestic sense as will be in terms of holiday travel so you may find yourself taking stock your life. July and August both bring ever-changing vistas and a great sense of self-belief, which is everything to your zodiac sign. Now is als the best time of the year to take on a new and unfamiliar challenge probably professional, but maybe personal.

September and October are probably the only two months of the ye during which you may be keeping a lower profile. It isn't that you fail get anything done, more that you are willing to watch and wait. This is good thing because it is right at the end of the year that you can bene the most by putting carefully laid plans into action. If not everyone seer to be supporting you at this time, it's up to you to bring them round strive to brush aside your instinctive reticence right now and take actio

The final months of the year, November and December, may just well carry the first breath of spring as far as you are concerned becau you will be just as lively as if this was the case. You seem to be on t form in just about every way and you can certainly make the most out an eventful and even quite magical Christmas and holiday period. Ke up your efforts right at the end of the year, because that will stand you good stead in the early months of next year.

January 2014

YOUR MONTH AT A GLANCE

✛ = Opportunities are around   ⬤ = Be on the defensive   ⬤ = Life is pretty ordinary

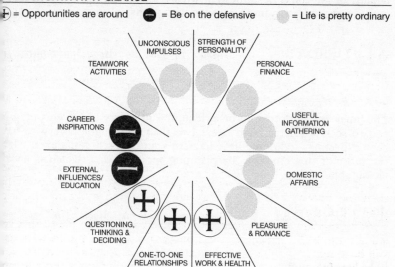

UNCONSCIOUS IMPULSES

STRENGTH OF PERSONALITY

TEAMWORK ACTIVITIES

PERSONAL FINANCE

CAREER INSPIRATIONS

USEFUL INFORMATION GATHERING

EXTERNAL INFLUENCES/ EDUCATION

DOMESTIC AFFAIRS

QUESTIONING, THINKING & DECIDING

ONE-TO-ONE RELATIONSHIPS

EFFECTIVE WORK & HEALTH

PLEASURE & ROMANCE

JANUARY HIGHS AND LOWS

Here I show you how the rhythms of the Moon will affect you this month. Like the tide, your energies and abilities will rise and fall with its pattern. When it is above the centre line, go for it, when it is below, you should be resting.

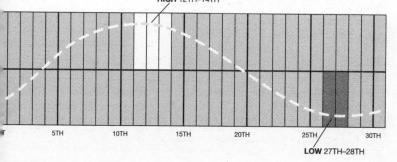

HIGH 12TH–14TH

5TH   10TH   15TH   20TH   25TH   30TH

LOW 27TH–28TH

30 MONDAY
Moon Age Day 28   Moon Sign Sagittarius

am ....

pm...

The lunar low arrives later today, which could persuade you to put the brakes on some of your plans for the next two or three days. At least you will get this slightly negative phase out of the way before the new year begins, but it could be somewhat frustrating all the same. It's simply a question of understanding your own limitations.

31 TUESDAY
Moon Age Day 29   Moon Sign Sagittarius

am ....

pm...

The lunar low can prove to be a disruptive influence today, encouraging you to seek a quieter New Year's Eve than you might otherwise have been expecting, and doing little to assist your own self-confidence. Make the most of this interlude by planning for next year, which is always pleasurable for you.

1 WEDNESDAY
Moon Age Day 0   Moon Sign Capricorn

am ....

pm...

A period of renewal is on offer, and it comes at a particularly good time, right at the beginning of a new year. The Sun is presently in your solar eighth house, where it stays until later in the month. You can't expect everything to stay the same, and in fact being a Gemini, you probably can't wait to start changing things.

2 THURSDAY
Moon Age Day 1   Moon Sign Capricorn

am ....

pm...

In terms of work there is little point in forcing issues now. Instead, you need to use as much tact and diplomacy as you possibly can. It's natural to be frustrated if people don't do things the way you wish. Remember that the world is filled with individuals, and allow for the variety you usually love so much.

YOUR DAILY GUIDE TO JANUARY 2014

FRIDAY *Moon Age Day 2 Moon Sign Aquarius*

....

....

ere's always a risk that information could unaccountably go astray
lay, unless you are scrupulous in the way you organise yourself. Geminis
not the tidiest people in the world, and there is the possibility that you
not giving matters your full attention. Bear in mind that one slight
stake now might mean hours putting things right at another time.

SATURDAY *Moon Age Day 3 Moon Sign Aquarius*

....

....

group matters can benefit from a spirit of harmony, and there never
s a better time to be getting on with just about anyone. You may be
htly less sure of yourself on a one-to-one basis, especially if you are
racting unwelcome attention. This would be an ideal time to welcome
ple you don't see very often back into your life again.

SUNDAY *Moon Age Day 4 Moon Sign Pisces*

....

....

e emphasis today is on doing everything you can to make life less
nplicated than it might otherwise be. Be prepared to simplify everything
1 can, which should enable you to be more organised and less stressed,
ticularly at work. If there's something you can't do, why not persuade
neone who knows better to lend a hand?

LOVE	MONEY	CAREER	VITALITY

+5 +4 +3 +2 +1 -1 -2 -3 -4 -5

6 MONDAY
Moon Age Day 5   Moon Sign Pi

am ....

pm...

Partners and loved ones can now be the source of emotional support wh
you need it most, and you can also tap into their excellent ideas. Lis
carefully to what they have to say, and act on it if it seems appropriate
your resources are running a little low, you need to address this situati
perhaps with the help of those close to you.

7 TUESDAY
Moon Age Day 6   Moon Sign A

am ....

pm...

This would be a very good time for seeking out places and faces you kn
and trust. Creative potential is to the fore, assisting you to get a real b
out of anything old, unusual or downright odd. It's time to show the v
zippy side of Gemini and to use it to demonstrate how wonderful you a

8 WEDNESDAY
Moon Age Day 7   Moon Sign A

am ....

pm...

The emphasis now is on your own ego, which might be rather too str
for your own good. All Gemini people mellow with age, but if you
young and headstrong you may need to put the brakes on now. Sometir
it pays to let others have the benefit of the doubt. It won't hurt you a
it could mean everything to them.

9 THURSDAY
Moon Age Day 8   Moon Sign A

am ....

pm...

This is a period during which the things you observe around you can
a source of great joy. The signs are that congratulations could be d
particularly in the family, and that celebrations are the order of the d
There are gains to be made by showing the world that you are far l
interested in yourself than usual at the moment.

10 FRIDAY
Moon Age Day 9   Moon Sign Taurus

m..

m..

Now is the time to think big and expect the best from life. A slightly quieter approach would be no bad thing, though that needn't stop you from displaying your magnetic personality and attracting plenty of attention from others. At work you have scope to make progress with any objectives that have been outstanding for some time.

11 SATURDAY
Moon Age Day 10   Moon Sign Taurus

m..

m..

Don't argue for your limitations today or you are likely to discover them even more. Instead, be confident and go for what you want. The Moon is in your solar twelfth house so a once again a quieter interlude is favoured, but you should soon be able to redress the balance. Make the most of any unexpected romantic possibilities that are on offer.

12 SUNDAY
Moon Age Day 11   Moon Sign Gemini

m..

m..

You have what it takes to make a success of whatever you decide to do today. It's about remaining positive and capitalising on the presence of the lunar high. If you are willing to seek help from others, and to show your free and easy spirit, the world can be your oyster in so many ways. Concern for the underdog is emphasised at present.

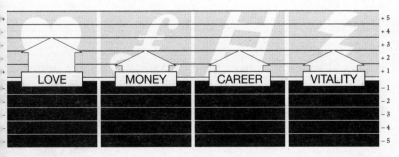

13 MONDAY
Moon Age Day 12   Moon Sign Gemini

am ....

pm ....

Another day of favourable influences on which you should be anxious to get ahead whenever you can. If things get a little sluggish by the afternoon, it's worth using your personal charm and determination to turn the tables. There will always be some people who aren't satisfied, and your best response is simply to ignore them if you can.

14 TUESDAY
Moon Age Day 13   Moon Sign Gemini

am ....

pm ....

Certain emotional matters could prove to be quite a bind today, though this is less likely if you make a definite decision to vary your routines and to push for a fun sort of day. There's nothing wrong with seeking people who are willing to lend a hand, since Gemini is rarely short of friends. Allow yourself to rely on them a little today.

15 WEDNESDAY
Moon Age Day 14   Moon Sign Cancer

am ....

pm ....

A fairly brisk pace with many comings and goings, both by you and by family members. Maybe there's some sort of celebration in the offing, but whatever is going on you need to find ways of enjoying yourself and help others to do the same. A Wednesday of fun is there for the taking, so don't be put off by anything.

16 THURSDAY
Moon Age Day 15   Moon Sign Cancer

am ....

pm ....

In a social sense the current trends encourage a positive attitude and you can afford to be the centre of whatever is going on in your vicinity. You have it within you to raise the spirits of anyone who is down in the dumps, and there is nothing more rewarding than that. Pointless family arguments are best avoided today.

17 FRIDAY

Moon Age Day 16   Moon Sign Leo

am ....

pm ....

Does it seem as though your influence over life is slightly on the wane today? If this is the case, you need to view this as a temporary matter. A little extra patience can work wonders, especially if you are dealing with family members who seem determined to be awkward. You might even decide that a domestic conference is called for.

18 SATURDAY

Moon Age Day 17   Moon Sign Leo

am ....

pm ....

Gemini has potential to be quite nostalgic today, which is fairly unusual for your zodiac sign. Present planetary trends encourage you to look back as much as forward, which is often thought to be quite a negative thing. Don't be so sure, though. You may be able to learn some lessons by replaying some situations.

19 SUNDAY

Moon Age Day 18   Moon Sign Leo

am ....

pm ....

Social contacts are well accented, assisting you to get on well with just about anyone. Of course, there will always be people who don't see life in the way you do, so you will need to have the patience to take their opinions on board too. There may be times at the moment when your brain is working faster than your hands can keep up!

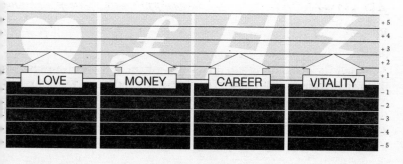

20 MONDAY
Moon Age Day 19   Moon Sign Vir

am ....

pm ....

It looks as though there is a great deal of progress to be made through the conversations you have around now, and you might be able to significant influence colleagues and superiors today. Be prepared to speak your min though once again it is important to display a degree of diplomacy if y can manage it.

21 TUESDAY
Moon Age Day 20   Moon Sign Vir

am ....

pm ....

Beware of getting involved in arguments if you can help it, but if you ha no choice make sure that you settle them quickly and efficiently. Yo ability to stand up to others is highlighted now, though this mightn't be side of your nature that you like to show very often. Right now, thoug it might be unavoidable!

22 WEDNESDAY
Moon Age Day 21   Moon Sign Libr

am ....

pm ....

The Sun is now in your solar ninth house, bringing a period during whi you have a chance to explore brand new ideas and philosophies. Y might decide to use this interlude to do something fresh and excitin particularly if you can free yourself from some of the restrictions that ha been around you for a while.

23 THURSDAY
Moon Age Day 22   Moon Sign Libr

am ....

pm ....

Although there should be no doubt that you are progressive right no there are occasions that demand a softly, softly approach. Knowing whe to be cool and casual isn't always very easy, and it's important that y read the signs that others are giving. Activities of a physical nature have great deal to offer you today.

4 FRIDAY
Moon Age Day 23   Moon Sign Scorpio

....

....

all means act with some confidence today, though the results may not
quite what you would expect or hope. Be generous in the way you deal
h colleagues, even if as far as you are concerned they don't really come
to scratch. By the evening you could be ready to sit in a chair and do
hing in particular.

5 SATURDAY
Moon Age Day 24   Moon Sign Scorpio

....

....

most situations you have room to take a more dominant role than
al this weekend. Group activities still have much to offer, though bear
mind that all groups must have a leader – and that leader could well be
u! A little more humility wouldn't go amiss, but that could be asking
her too much.

6 SUNDAY
Moon Age Day 25   Moon Sign Scorpio

....

....

sitive highlights come along in terms of all leisure and romance. Pleasing
urself is the name of the game on what is, after all, a Sunday. Short
tings or trips with friends have a great deal of potential for pleasure,
d events today should offer you plenty of new ideas, which you can use
achieve practical advancement in the future.

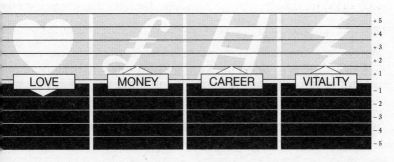

47

27 MONDAY *Moon Age Day 26   Moon Sign Sagittar*

am ....

pm ....

Acting on impulse is not to be recommended during the lunar low, a
it would probably be much better for yourself and all concerned if y
seek advice from those who know better than you do. Even if you a
determined to push on with specific jobs, it might seem as if you a
walking through treacle. A little patience is called for.

28 TUESDAY *Moon Age Day 27   Moon Sign Sagittar*

am ....

pm ....

Once again, a more inward-looking Gemini is indicated, though y
needn't allow the world at large to notice this fact at all. Routines probal
suit you better now than would normally be the case, and this would
an ideal time to get any tedious jobs out of the way. Who knows, und
current influences you might even enjoy it!

29 WEDNESDAY *Moon Age Day 28   Moon Sign Caprico*

am ....

pm ....

A quieter approach works early in the day, but later on you should
looking for opportunities to get things going with a real buzz. Y
needn't take no for an answer if you know in your heart that your opini
is correct, and this advice may be particularly appropriate for domes
issues. Confidence is not lacking, and diplomacy is your middle name.

30 THURSDAY *Moon Age Day 29   Moon Sign Caprico*

am ....

pm ....

Trends assist you to be on top form today. It's time to demonstrate th
you are good company, and that you don't have any difficulties maki
new friends or keeping the ones you already have. Acting on impulse
very much a part of who you are, and this should come as no surprise
anyone. People should find you refreshing to be around now.

1 FRIDAY   *Moon Age Day 0   Moon Sign Aquarius*

n...

n...

he weekend is not here yet, and it's worth making one extra push to get
ings moving the way you would wish with regard to your work. There is
uch to be said for telling superiors how you feel about a specific matter,
articularly if you use your current tact and make sure you sprinkle your
omments with compliments.

SATURDAY   *Moon Age Day 1   Moon Sign Aquarius*

n...

m...

ow you can see how much luck you have on your side by embarking
n a number of different projects. Although the morning is better than
ter in the day for business, social prospects continue to look favourable
ntil bedtime. Make the most of the romantic potential that is available,
ossibly from an unexpected source.

SUNDAY   *Moon Age Day 2   Moon Sign Pisces*

n...

m...

here are gains to be made in the financial arena, particularly if you can
apitalise on decisions you made some time ago, or maybe take advantage
f the generosity of those around you. Your need to feel secure at home,
hich might mean thinking about some changes. Gemini has scope to
ake this a distinctly creative period.

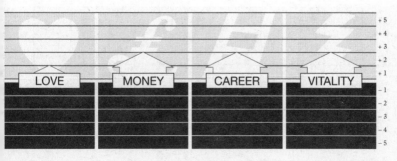

49

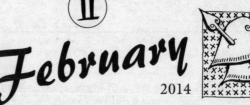

♊ February 2014

YOUR MONTH AT A GLANCE

$\oplus$ = Opportunities are around $\ominus$ = Be on the defensive   ○ = Life is pretty ordina

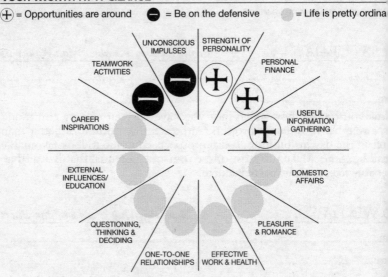

FEBRUARY HIGHS AND LOWS

Here I show you how the rhythms of the Moon will affect you this month Like the tide, your energies and abilities will rise and fall with its patter When it is above the centre line, go for it, when it is below, you shoul be resting.

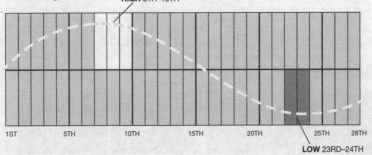

50

MONDAY
Moon Age Day 3   Moon Sign Pisces

n...

n...

ntellectual exchanges are now your forte, and – typical of your sign – you ke to mix with as many different types of people as you possibly can. ather than being ruled by the past, it's important to push your mind orward at every opportunity. If you don't want the things you are saying be misconstrued, make sure you explain yourself fully.

TUESDAY
Moon Age Day 4   Moon Sign Aries

n...

n...

rends encourage you to take care with the feelings of others today, and pecially those of your partner. If you have been particularly busy of late, iis would be an ideal time to slow things down a little, however difficult iat seems. Ask yourself whether it's really worth crossing swords with eople over petty issues that don't matter at all.

WEDNESDAY
Moon Age Day 5   Moon Sign Aries

n...

m...

ou have a great desire to restructure your life in some way, and with enus in its present position this could well have something to do with lationships. There is more romantic verve available, and you can use this breathe new life into existing attachments. Take note of the positive esponses you get from the individuals concerned.

THURSDAY
Moon Age Day 6   Moon Sign Taurus

n...

m...

iscussions associated with travel are well starred today, and those of ou actually making journeys at this time can benefit as a result. Keep our business head on at work and don't allow sentiment to get in the ay of practical progress. Finances can be strengthened as the weekend pproaches, even if only marginally so.

7 FRIDAY ☿ *Moon Age Day 7 Moon Sign Taur*

am...

pm...

Today would be a great time to settle any issues that have been outstandir for quite a while. For the moment it is important to avoid argumen and to do whatever you can to be a peacemaker and a general hone broker. This is also a favourable time for finding time to make conta with anyone you don't see very often.

8 SATURDAY ☿ *Moon Age Day 8 Moon Sign Gemi*

am...

pm...

You have what it takes to make sure there's plenty happening today, ar the present position of the Moon is a great support to you. The lun high offers popularity, and perhaps even notoriety for some. Romant overturns are the order of the day for Gemini, and you also ought to l tapping into some luck in the money stakes.

9 SUNDAY ☿ *Moon Age Day 9 Moon Sign Gemi*

am...

pm...

Another potentially positive day for Gemini, but it pays to be just a litt diplomatic with anyone who is not quite as dynamic as you are. Spur-c the-moment decisions can certainly work in your favour, and you m find that you are able to turn heads in a romantic sense. You have sco to make this one of the best days of the month.

	LOVE	MONEY	CAREER	VITALITY

10 MONDAY ☿ *Moon Age Day 10   Moon Sign Gemini*

m..

m..

The lunar low begins to retreat, bringing a period of emotional ups and downs. Your best approach is to play things cool and avoid getting involved in arguments that are not of your making. Is someone you know well in need of a little moral support at this time? Perhaps you are in just the right position to offer it.

11 TUESDAY ☿ *Moon Age Day 11   Moon Sign Cancer*

m..

m..

You needn't allow much to steer you off course today, and the planetary line-up looks especially promising. This part of the week offers a higher degree of excitement than was possible even during the recent lunar high. Even if family arrangements have to be altered, it's up to you to rise to any occasion.

12 WEDNESDAY ☿ *Moon Age Day 12   Moon Sign Cancer*

m..

m..

Maintaining a high degree of confidence is all very well, but it's possible to take this a little too far for your own good. Take situations one at a time and wait for more promising times before you take any irrevocable decisions. The quieter side of your nature is highlighted, and creative activities would be an excellent outlet.

13 THURSDAY ☿ *Moon Age Day 13   Moon Sign Leo*

m..

m..

If you give way to excessive optimism now, there's a risk you could find yourself coming unstuck. Today works best if you remain rather critical, if anything, and don't necessarily believe everything you either read or are told. The path to success may be a little harder during this part of the week, but it's still well marked for many of you.

53

14 FRIDAY ☿ *Moon Age Day 14 Moon Sign Le*

am...

pm...

All things domestic offer scope for plenty of fulfilment today, encouraging you to turn away from strictly professional matters at this stage of the week. There's nothing wrong with allowing others to take some of the strain while you enjoy some time to yourself. Confidence is everything when it comes to new pursuits.

15 SATURDAY ☿ *Moon Age Day 15 Moon Sign Le*

am...

pm...

Diplomacy counts for a great deal now, so it's worth taking particular care with the way you are dealing with others. It's important to explain yourself fully, and this should help your efforts to come to terms with the needs of family members and your partner. It's all too easy to be caustic without realising the fact.

16 SUNDAY ☿ *Moon Age Day 16 Moon Sign Virg*

am...

pm...

Be prepared to pursue some long-term objectives today, and to seek assistance from those around you if you need it. This may not be the best time to go it alone, and if other people are willing to give you support you might as well accept it. The slightly awkward side of your nature is emphasised right now.

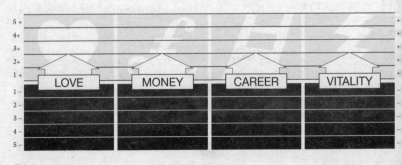

17 MONDAY ☿ *Moon Age Day 17   Moon Sign Virgo*

am ....

pm ....

You are in a good position to influence the way others are thinking, even if you don't necessarily have what it takes to get ahead yourself. One area of life that does hold positive potential is romance, and you also need to look for chances to impress someone at work, though this may not have been your original intention.

18 TUESDAY ☿ *Moon Age Day 18   Moon Sign Libra*

am ....

pm ....

There are times when as a Gemini you are inclined to speak without thinking as much as you should. The best way to avoid this is to use a little tact and diplomacy, which could save you from having to apologise quite so much! A day to maintain your popularity among friends, and to capitalise on favourable social prospects.

19 WEDNESDAY ☿ *Moon Age Day 19   Moon Sign Libra*

am ....

pm ....

The spotlight is on the energy and enthusiasm you put into your life at the moment, and the planetary trends surrounding you can definitely assist you significantly. It's fine for younger family members to please themselves, but that needn't stop you from keeping a watchful eye over them all the same. There's a fine balance to strike in terms of discipline.

20 THURSDAY ☿ *Moon Age Day 20   Moon Sign Libra*

am ....

pm ....

It may be hard to keep your mind on a particular subject today, especially if it is something that bores you. You can afford to be in the market for enjoyment, and to join forces with people who share a similar view. Don't forget your family responsibilities, but look for ways to incorporate these into your social needs.

21 FRIDAY ☿ *Moon Age Day 21   Moon Sign Scorpi*

am..

pm..

You have what it takes to achieve a good deal of financial stability in you
life right now, which isn't always the case for your zodiac sign. A mello
approach works well for Gemini at present, and this should allow yo
to take notice of any situations you have ignored recently. Creating
positive atmosphere among friends can work wonders.

22 SATURDAY ☿ *Moon Age Day 22   Moon Sign Scorpi*

am..

pm..

Although there may be a slight tendency to think about number one a
this stage of the month, you should be able to overcome this becaus
your compassion is to the fore. Now is the time to demonstrate how loya
you are to your friends and to go that extra mile on their behalf. Romanc
is likely to throw up some interesting possibilities now.

23 SUNDAY ☿ *Moon Age Day 23   Moon Sign Sagittariu*

am..

pm..

The arrival of the lunar low could bring a slight element of stress t
certain tasks you have to undertake today, but if you keep smiling yo
should hardly notice this fact. Seeking support from friends would be n
bad thing, and this might even assist your financial progress. Why no
have some fun in the evening?

	LOVE	MONEY	CAREER	VITALITY
5 +				
4+				
3+				
2+				
1 +				
1 -				
2 -				
3 -				
4 -				
5 -				

4 MONDAY   ☿ *Moon Age Day 24   Moon Sign Sagittarius*

....

....

hough today might not be any luckier in a general sense than yesterday
ned out to be, you can afford to be in the market for a bargain or two.
e lunar low is not the ideal time to be signing documents if you can
oid it. If you have no choice, make certain you read any small print as
efully as possible.

5 TUESDAY   ☿ *Moon Age Day 25   Moon Sign Capricorn*

....

....

day to discuss all issues in order to enlist a little help. This should enable
u to get plans off to an amazing start, at a time when you stand a good
ance of bringing them to fruition. Red tape is best avoided now, and
s worth making certain that you can move in a certain direction before
u even get your skates on.

6 WEDNESDAY   ☿ *Moon Age Day 26   Moon Sign Capricorn*

....

....

ok out for work situations that can put you in the picture and lead to
ther advances of a sort you might not have been expecting. There are
ny surprises on offer at the moment, and this justifies the confidence
u have had in yourself recently. Creative potential also seems well
rked at the moment.

7 THURSDAY   ☿ *Moon Age Day 27   Moon Sign Aquarius*

....

....

favourable trend is available in a domestic sense, even if you are finding
e outside world just a little unsettling at times. For this reason you
y decide to stick to your home surroundings, where you should feel
tremely secure. This is out of kilter with the usual Gemini attitude, but
ould only be a temporary matter.

28 FRIDAY

☿ *Moon Age Day 28   Moon Sign Aquari*

am...

pm...

Friendship and teamwork matters are positively highlighted under prese
trends, particularly as they relate to your social life. Make today your ov
as much as proves to be possible and allow the slightly competitive side
your nature to shine through, even if you are aiming to be a team play
at the moment.

1 SATURDAY

Moon Age Day 0   Moon Sign Pis

am...

pm...

A new month dawns, and with it the awareness that spring is just arou
the corner. That should cheer you up no end, because it's a season th
has a great deal to offer. It's time to get out there in the social mainstrea
and make an impact on the world at large. Romance could well be a maj
factor in your life soon.

2 SUNDAY

Moon Age Day 1   Moon Sign Pis

am...

pm...

There is a great opportunity today to broaden your horizons in so
way. Travel and mental pursuits of all sorts are to the fore at the mome
and the focus is also on the inquisitive side of your nature. There may
good reasons to seek support from others around now, particularly fam
members, so don't be reluctant to do so.

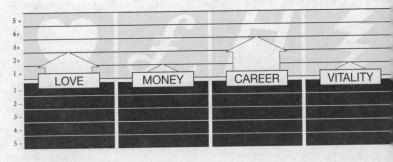

March

2014

UR MONTH AT A GLANCE

= Opportunities are around   ⬤ = Be on the defensive   ⬤ = Life is pretty ordinary

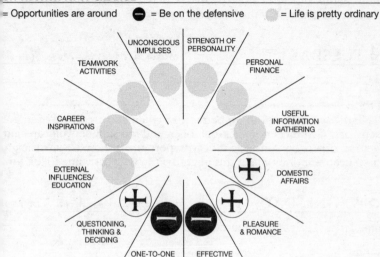

ARCH HIGHS AND LOWS

re I show you how the rhythms of the Moon will affect you this month. e the tide, your energies and abilities will rise and fall with its pattern. en it is above the centre line, go for it, when it is below, you should resting.

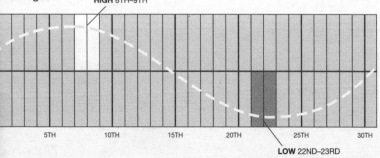

3 MONDAY
Moon Age Day 2   Moon Sign Ar

am ....

pm...

Career objectives are highlighted now, so it makes sense to devote a go
deal of your attention to this sphere of your life. Family concerns –
you have any – might have to be left on the back burner for a few hou
though that shouldn't stop you from gaining support and assistance fr
a particular friendship this evening.

4 TUESDAY
Moon Age Day 3   Moon Sign Ar

am ....

pm...

Things have potential to go better now when you are involved in gro
activities. Gemini is not a natural loner, and the support you can gain
getting others on your side is very important. If there is something y
have been wanting of late, this might be the very best time to ask for i

5 WEDNESDAY
Moon Age Day 4   Moon Sign Tau

am ....

pm...

There should be help around if you want it, and even if you don't, do y
really need to let anyone know? Success today is about showing that y
are good to know, inspirational in relationships and warm to your frien
Conversation counts for a great deal now, and can allow you to addr
the worries that others find difficult to express.

6 THURSDAY
Moon Age Day 5   Moon Sign Tau

am ....

pm...

It pays to make an early start today and deal immediately with ideas th
have just come off the drawing board of your busy mind. Later in the c
you can afford to relax, a process that won't be at all easy if you are s
trying to solve those last little problems. The early bird really does ca
the worm today.

FRIDAY
Moon Age Day 6   Moon Sign Taurus

....

....

...day mainly centres on matters of private concern. Your need for ...usion is emphasised while the Moon occupies your solar twelfth ...se. A cautious approach to business is recommended for the moment, ... if you decide to take some time off from responsibilities generally, so ...ch the better. Be ready to capitalise on more positive days to come.

SATURDAY
Moon Age Day 7   Moon Sign Gemini

....

....

...should now be taking advantage of all the luck that is on your side, ... exploiting it for all you are worth. The lunar high also encourages ... to display the sporting side of Gemini, and this in turn should help ... to get yourself noticed by others. Finding time for social activities is ... important, if somewhat difficult!

SUNDAY
Moon Age Day 8   Moon Sign Gemini

....

....

...lunar high continues, giving you everything you need to put yourself ...he right place to make significant progress. Speaking your mind can ...lly make the difference, and you mightn't take too much persuading ...do this. Your dealings are all above-board and the amount of trust you ... gain is noteworthy. Popularity is also well marked.

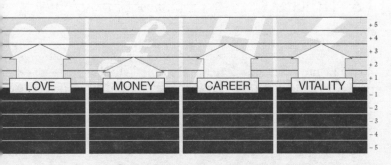

61

10 MONDAY
Moon Age Day 9   Moon Sign Can

am ....

pm ....

When it comes to the social side of life, you need to show that you are your very best now. It shouldn't be hard for you to modify your nature suit that of others, and you have a definite ability to adapt in a mome by-moment sense. Intellectually speaking, trends assist you to be on t form around this time.

11 TUESDAY
Moon Age Day 10   Moon Sign Can

am ....

pm ....

A rather assertive and even argumentative phase is indicated around no The problem is that you know how things should be done, and may n have too much patience with those who refuse to accept your point view. Bear in mind that a difference of opinion could lead to argumen which will be counter-productive.

12 WEDNESDAY
Moon Age Day 11   Moon Sign Can

am ....

pm ....

Being popular takes effort right now, which is why it might sometim seem simpler to stick to your own company. Everyone deserves a qu time now and again, and this clearly includes Gemini. Even if friends warm and helpful, it could simply be that you don't want them arou too much for today.

13 THURSDAY
Moon Age Day 12   Moon Sign

am ....

pm ....

Romantic prospects look better as the Moon changes its house positi With plenty of love to offer those who are important to you, there is reason to hold back on your Gemini ability to find the right words. more practical situations it's worth calling upon the help of someone w is definitely in the know.

4 FRIDAY
Moon Age Day 13   Moon Sign Leo

....

....

here is one thing that is really likely to make you enthusiastic at the ment, it is the possibility of travel. You need fresh fields and pastures v and won't be too inclined to stick around the house this Friday. If have to be in one place, or are working, it is your fertile imagination t offers the stimulation you need.

5 SATURDAY
Moon Age Day 14   Moon Sign Virgo

....

....

es it seem that there are people around this weekend who exist in ler to test your patience? The best way forward is very clear, though icult to follow – don't rise to the bait! The more calm and collected you nain, the greater is the chance you will bring even the most awkward ts round to your point of view.

6 SUNDAY
Moon Age Day 15   Moon Sign Virgo

....

....

e most favourable trends for this Sunday seem to surround home and iily. Acting on impulse now comes as second nature, and this makes ess likely that you'll be laying down hard-and-fast plans at this time. ooting from the hip is all very well, but take care because there is a ;ht possibility that you could make mistakes.

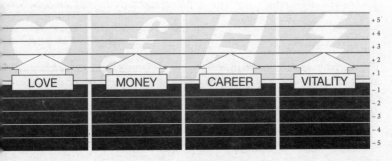

17 MONDAY
Moon Age Day 16   Moon Sign Vir

am...

pm...

There could be a real test of strength on the work front today, and y
will have to stick to your guns. That's not usually difficult for your zod
sign, but at the same time it is important to keep an air of diplomacy. Y
can afford to let your confidence grow as you embark on projects th
really suit you this week.

18 TUESDAY
Moon Age Day 17   Moon Sign Lib

am...

pm...

Once again, confidence is now well accented, assisting you to mak
good impression. Persuading colleagues to listen to your point of vi
is the first step towards convincing them to follow your lead in vari
situations. If conventional ways of doing things don't appeal, make su
you show your individuality!

19 WEDNESDAY
Moon Age Day 18   Moon Sign Lib

am...

pm...

There are challenges around, though that shouldn't bother you in t
slightest. Getting on with those close to you is now child's play, particula
if you show the charming side of your nature even more strongly th
usual. Attitude is important when you are thinking about approachi
someone in the family regarding a specific issue.

20 THURSDAY
Moon Age Day 19   Moon Sign Scor

am...

pm...

The social side of your nature remains uppermost at this time, thoug
touch of restlessness can't be ruled out. Your best approach is to tac
a variety of things in order to avoid becoming bored with your lot. T
to get out and take a look at the seasons changing first hand. Coast
country – it doesn't matter. It's the break that counts.

21 FRIDAY
Moon Age Day 20   Moon Sign Scorpio

am ....

pm...

There is increased creativity available to you now, making this an excellent time to think about the sort of changes you want to make at home. Firing up the enthusiasm of people in your family shouldn't be too difficult, specially in the case of younger individuals with whom you have forged particular connection.

22 SATURDAY
Moon Age Day 21   Moon Sign Sagittarius

m ....

m...

The lunar low encourages an element of irritation if you can't do exactly what you want, when you wish to do it. However, if you realise that present trends are not geared towards material success, you can at least put some of your schemes on hold and still have a good day. It's all a matter of looking at priorities.

23 SUNDAY
Moon Age Day 22   Moon Sign Sagittarius

m ....

m...

Delays are a distinct possibility now as the lunar low continues. It could well feel as though your strength has diminished, and that progress is difficult to achieve. Your best approach is to avoid taking on too much and give yourself time for a break. You still have the ability to maintain your popularity, and that should be reassuring.

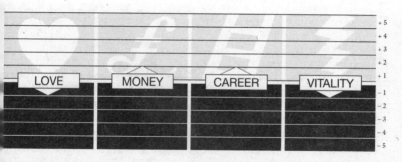

24 MONDAY   *Moon Age Day 23   Moon Sign Capricorn*

am ....

pm..

You could well feel that you are shooting out of a cannon as you emerge from the lunar low into the full glare of the Sun in your solar eleventh house. The spotlight is clearly on social demands for now, and you'll need to be ready to focus your attention in various directions. Your natural enthusiasm and optimism should be back in place.

25 TUESDAY   *Moon Age Day 24   Moon Sign Capricorn*

am ....

pm..

Romance seems to be the special key to happiness around now, and you have scope to gain particular satisfaction with the way your personal life is panning out. You can't expect everyone to think you are wonderful and in the case of people who don't, your best approach is to shrug your shoulders and simply accept the fact.

26 WEDNESDAY   *Moon Age Day 25   Moon Sign Aquarius*

am ....

pm..

There are strong stimulating influences that allow you to move closer to your heart's desire than might have been the case for quite a while. Even if you can't achieve everything you would wish, you can at least demonstrate a higher degree of patience than is usually the case. The most attractive side of Gemini should now be on show to others.

27 THURSDAY   *Moon Age Day 26   Moon Sign Aquarius*

am ....

pm..

Getting your message across certainly isn't likely to be a problem for you now. On the contrary, you have what it takes to express yourself better than ever, and should find you can make significant gains as a result. Look out for personalities, and make the most of the chance to meet interesting people throughout the day.

8 FRIDAY
Moon Age Day 27   Moon Sign Aquarius

n ....

n ....

hat you could well be seeking at the end of this working week is a
eater opportunity to please yourself. Being pushed into situations that
on't interest you is unlikely to appeal, and your boredom threshold
on't be at its highest. Perhaps it's time to find someone who can be
rsuaded to at least share the tedious jobs.

9 SATURDAY
Moon Age Day 28   Moon Sign Pisces

n ....

n ....

etting others on your side should be within your abilities, and is quite
portant at the moment. Showing yourself to be a good team player
part of this process, though as usual, this works best when you are in
arge of the team. Don't be too quick to apportion blame if something
es wrong. After all – it might end up being your fault!

0 SUNDAY
Moon Age Day 29   Moon Sign Pisces

n ....

n ....

's time to show a distinctly optimistic face to the world at large and to
monstrate what great fun you are to be with today. It doesn't matter
hether you are entertaining your partner, family or friends. Gemini can
naturally showy, and should relish being the centre of attention. Make
e most of any good spring weather.

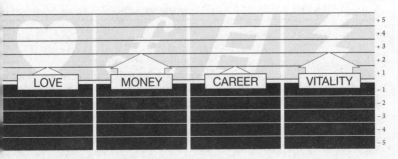

31 MONDAY
Moon Age Day 0   Moon Sign Ar

am ....

pm..

Trends indicate that romance is going to be positively highlighted in yo
life around now. Although you clearly have what it takes to turn hea
you could inspire a little jealousy without intending to do so. Bargains a
all well and good, but beware of impulse buys that might not be quite
good as they first appear.

1 TUESDAY
Moon Age Day 1   Moon Sign Ar

am ....

pm..

The odd setback is possible where social arrangements are concerne
which in itself could be somewhat irritating. On the whole, however, t
planets line up to offer reasonable influences for you at this stage of t
working week. Nevertheless, this isn't the ideal time to rush into putti
brand new plans into action at work.

2 WEDNESDAY
Moon Age Day 2   Moon Sign Taur

am ....

pm..

The spotlight is on important discussions today, though you need
avoid them turning into disputes and should make that fact as clear as y
can, early in the day. Preparation counts for a great deal now, particula
if you are facing some kind of test or examination in the near futu
Concentration is the key today.

3 THURSDAY
Moon Age Day 3   Moon Sign Taur

am ....

pm..

Unconventionality should be the order of the day, both in your choi
of people to mix with, and in your determination not to settle for a ru
of-the-mill sort of Thursday. The more excitement you can pack in, t
greater is the enjoyment you can derive from life. Beware of being t
quick to jump to conclusions in personal attachments.

4 FRIDAY
Moon Age Day 4   Moon Sign Gemini

m ....

m ....

The lunar high gives you all the assistance you need to make a good impression and to take on as many new projects as possible. It's time to show the deeper side of your nature, and to use it to influence and please those with whom you come into contact. You might even find it possible to approach a superior on an equal footing.

5 SATURDAY
Moon Age Day 5   Moon Sign Gemini

m ....

m ....

Physical and emotional strengths are at a peak, allowing you to feel good and to act with significant determination. Don't be too quick to jump to negative conclusions, because the lunar high is very supportive in most spheres of your life. What might matter most to you at present is maintaining your tremendous popularity.

6 SUNDAY
Moon Age Day 6   Moon Sign Cancer

m ....

m ....

Gemini is never afraid to push matters to the brink of disaster in search of success, which takes a great deal out of your nerves and it's worth asking whether this is really necessary. It would be much better to plan slowly and steadily for any future challenges. In your personal life be ready to explain the way you feel before you are asked.

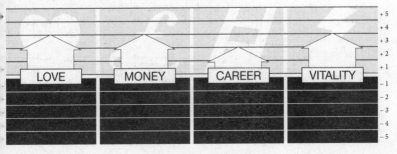

April

2014

YOUR MONTH AT A GLANCE

(+) = Opportunities are around   ⊖ = Be on the defensive   ● = Life is pretty ordina

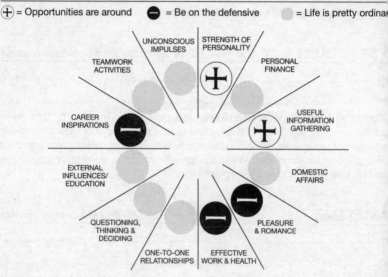

APRIL HIGHS AND LOWS

Here I show you how the rhythms of the Moon will affect you this month. Like the tide, your energies and abilities will rise and fall with its pattern. When it is above the centre line, go for it, when it is below, you should be resting.

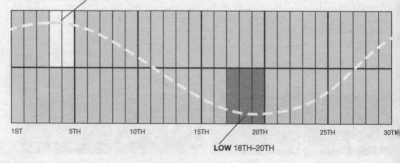

HIGH 4TH–5TH

LOW 18TH–20TH

7 MONDAY
Moon Age Day 7   Moon Sign Cancer

m..

m..

. new change of emphasis at work could well find you busier than ever, though it may prove difficult to address everything that seems important right now. Do some of those around you seem to be behaving out of character? Your best response to such a situation is to adopt a careful and considered approach.

8 TUESDAY
Moon Age Day 8   Moon Sign Cancer

m..

m..

s is often the case with Gemini, your ability to convince others is second to none today, making it more likely that neither your knowledge nor the way you put it across are called into question. The sheer magnetism of our nature can help you to increase your popularity, and you should have no difficulty bringing people round to your own opinions.

9 WEDNESDAY
Moon Age Day 9   Moon Sign Leo

m..

m..

ocial trends are on the up, and some of the negative qualities that have been around for some of you should now be blown away on a breeze of optimism. You can afford to put comfort and security on the back burner and take a few risks as you capitalise on the first of a series of astrological trends that stimulate your desire to travel.

10 THURSDAY
Moon Age Day 10   Moon Sign Leo

m..

m..

What matters most of all today is that avenues of communication are wide open to you. The more you choose to get out and about today, the greater will be the rewards that you can reap. There's an emphasis on looking right today, and a good attitude towards presentation is genuinely of significance at this time.

11 FRIDAY
Moon Age Day 11   Moon Sign Vir

am...

pm...

Your ability to make improvements to the smooth-running of plans is th main thing that sets today apart. Although life may not exactly be tedio right now, it might not be especially exciting either. Of course, there nothing at all to prevent you from putting in that extra bit of effort th will count – so get cracking!

12 SATURDAY
Moon Age Day 12   Moon Sign Vir

am...

pm...

Socially speaking, you have what it takes to elicit some positive respons from others at the moment. It terms of finances, you might have slight more scope to make some progress, though that doesn't necessarily me you will be feeling rich. Ideas from the past can be brought to fruiti under current planetary influences.

13 SUNDAY
Moon Age Day 13   Moon Sign Vir

am...

pm...

Social events are particularly well highlighted and remain so for the ne couple of days. This would be an ideal time to focus on those close you, and to ensure they feel special, particularly if they have been dov for some reason. There is a very selfless feel to Gemini at present, whi others should appreciate.

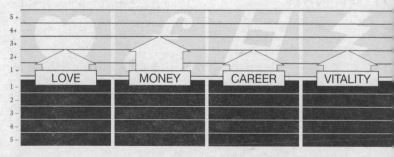

4 MONDAY   *Moon Age Day 14   Moon Sign Libra*

....

....

nce again you have potential to make ground in social developments, ough the real emphasis of the day is on work matters. After a weekend at offered opportunities for relaxation, you are now in a position to sh yourself fairly hard. You can't expect everyone to have your best terests at heart, so be willing to use your intuition.

5 TUESDAY   *Moon Age Day 15   Moon Sign Libra*

....

....

ne tendency towards being easily bored is highlighted, which is why would be sensible to indulge in as many different activities as you can ght now. Be prepared to deal with confidences from a whole range of rections. You might even feel that you know more about the private es of others than you do about your own!

6 WEDNESDAY   *Moon Age Day 16   Moon Sign Scorpio*

....

....

his would be a very favourable interlude for pursuing important scussions and for making up your mind to get on with any situations at have been waiting around for some time. There's nothing wrong th seeking out help when you need it the most. All the more reason to ake a beeline for some well-meaning friends.

7 THURSDAY   *Moon Age Day 17   Moon Sign Scorpio*

....

....

a professional sense you should now be able to get things going with swing. If there isn't quite as much time to spend with your loved ones you would wish, you can take heart and ensure that you remedy that tuation later. There are signs that someone who is above you in the ecking order could be especially useful today.

♊

18 FRIDAY
Moon Age Day 18   Moon Sign Sagittar

am..

pm..

Practical issues are subject to the sort of limitations that come alo
when the Moon is in your opposite zodiac sign, leading to a potentia
problematical day. Your best response is to stay away from trying
organise things too much and concentrate on relaxation. It is entir
possible that in this way you'll fail to even recognise the lunar low.

19 SATURDAY
Moon Age Day 19   Moon Sign Sagittar

am..

pm..

Be prepared for your ideas and views to be challenged in some way tod
If this occurs, it's important that you keep your cool and that you do
react too harshly to any situation. The time you choose to spend at ho
counts for a great deal now that the weekend has arrived. Roman
inclinations are also emphasised.

20 SUNDAY
Moon Age Day 20   Moon Sign Sagittar

am..

pm..

Although your patience could easily be tested in some way today, in t
main you should be able to start moving away from the negative tren
indicated by the lunar low and see the way ahead very clearly. There a
good reasons to offer some genuine Gemini assistance to the peop
around you who need it.

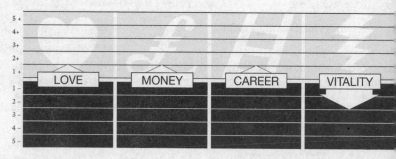

1 MONDAY
Moon Age Day 21   Moon Sign Capricorn

....

....

:ious material objectives seem to have success written all over them
this time, and you shouldn't find it difficult to forge ahead, even
:aking down a few barriers that might have seemed difficult to get over
·viously. Why not give yourself a chance to shine socially by accepting
· interesting invitations that are on offer?

2 TUESDAY
Moon Age Day 22   Moon Sign Capricorn

....

....

k yourself whether your style of debate at the moment might be a little
) sharp for others. If so, perhaps it would be sensible to tone down
ur approaches a little. Gemini can be one of the most diplomatic zodiac
ns, though this is less likely to be the case right now. Some patience is
cessary when dealing with less than positive types.

3 WEDNESDAY
Moon Age Day 23   Moon Sign Aquarius

....

....

a sharp contrast to yesterday, you now have what it takes to show
:at sensitivity and understanding when it matters the most. You are
:couraged by advancing planetary trends to put the more brash qualities
it have been in evidence of late on the back burner. Communication is
ll starred, and you have scope to boost your popularity.

4 THURSDAY
Moon Age Day 24   Moon Sign Aquarius

....

....

ogress today is a question of alternating times of withdrawal with
·ergetic social activity, creating the sort of balance that is more or less
:ond nature to you at this time. This means showing your sensitive side,
ile maintaining your drive and certainty. All in all you can present what
probably your best attitude of the whole month.

25 FRIDAY
Moon Age Day 25   Moon Sign Pis

am ....

pm...

Work issues almost guarantee good things coming your way at t
moment. Make an early start with new projects and don't give in to
natural laziness that seems to descend on you at some time today. Eve
seem to come along at the moment that can certainly help your love li

26 SATURDAY
Moon Age Day 26   Moon Sign Pis

am ....

pm...

Look out for a period of potential upheaval, but a time that allows you
dump anything that you feel is not working for you as it should. The
isn't much time for regrets, even though Gemini can be a soft-heart
zodiac sign. Once you have made up your mind to a particular course
action, conclusions become inevitable.

27 SUNDAY
Moon Age Day 27   Moon Sign Ar

am ....

pm...

Objectives that are at the drawing-board stage right now could well ne
some extra thinking before you can really put them into practice. W
not get in touch with individuals whose opinions you value and se
their views on current situations? New job opportunities are a distin
possibility, and Geminis really should be capitalising on them wherev
possible.

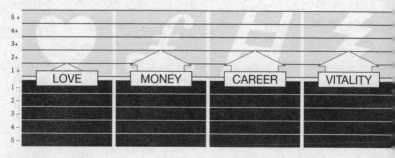

28 MONDAY
Moon Age Day 28   Moon Sign Aries

am ....

pm...

Where professional matters are concerned, the planetary picture today can indicate both mishaps and delays. Some patience is therefore necessary at the start of this working week. The social scene looks much more positive, though this is not really the sort of day when you should be taking on too much in the way of responsibility.

29 TUESDAY
Moon Age Day 29   Moon Sign Taurus

am ....

pm...

On a mundane level this would be a good day to focus specifically on your work and on the longer-term future. Career issues may be the most important ones at present, but they need not be your only concern. Later in the day there should be plenty of time to think about having fun, which is also very important at the moment.

30 WEDNESDAY
Moon Age Day 0   Moon Sign Taurus

am ....

pm...

There is good scope for getting ahead, though you are encouraged to think of more unusual ways to achieve this. Give yourself a chance to have a break as well, because all work and no play can make Gemini a dull girl or boy! The support you can elicit from others right now can really make the difference to your progress.

1 THURSDAY
Moon Age Day 1   Moon Sign Gemini

am ....

pm...

You should be taking full advantage of Lady Luck at the moment. The lunar high offers you new challenges but also the wherewithal to deal with them. There are few mountains too hard for Gemini to contemplate while the Moon is in your zodiac sign, and your determination to do what pleases you the most is definitely to the fore.

2 FRIDAY
Moon Age Day 2   Moon Sign Gemini

am...

pm...

With the lunar high now prompting you to take centre stage, you are occupying a much more favourable position generally than has been the case for a while. The Sun is approaching its best position of the year for you and the green light is on to go out and get exactly what you want from life.

3 SATURDAY
Moon Age Day 3   Moon Sign Gemini

am...

pm...

A potentially very hectic phase is on offer, though it is one that more or less demands you keep up with all the news and views in your vicinity. A degree of success could well be staring you in the face, possibly as a result of things you did in the past. Being certain of yourself is part of what makes today special.

4 SUNDAY
Moon Age Day 4   Moon Sign Cancer

am...

pm...

Your happiest interlude at the moment seem to be when you are in groups, where you have a chance to discover a certain sort of freedom and the level of support that could be lacking in other areas of your life. It's time to be determined in practical issues and to push forward with ideas, even if not everyone agrees with you.

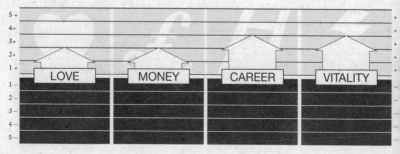

May

2014

OUR MONTH AT A GLANCE

= Opportunities are around   ⊖ = Be on the defensive   ⬤ = Life is pretty ordinary

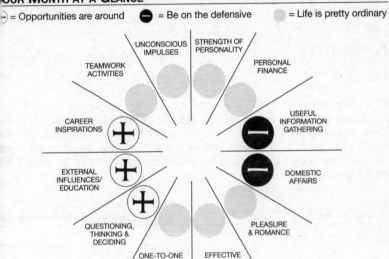

UNCONSCIOUS IMPULSES

STRENGTH OF PERSONALITY

TEAMWORK ACTIVITIES

PERSONAL FINANCE

CAREER INSPIRATIONS

USEFUL INFORMATION GATHERING

EXTERNAL INFLUENCES/ EDUCATION

DOMESTIC AFFAIRS

QUESTIONING, THINKING & DECIDING

PLEASURE & ROMANCE

ONE-TO-ONE RELATIONSHIPS

EFFECTIVE WORK & HEALTH

MAY HIGHS AND LOWS

Here I show you how the rhythms of the Moon will affect you this month. Like the tide, your energies and abilities will rise and fall with its pattern. When it is above the centre line, go for it, when it is below, you should be resting.

HIGH 1ST–3RD

HIGH 29TH–30TH

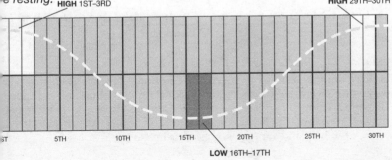

1ST   5TH   10TH   15TH   20TH   25TH   30TH

LOW 16TH–17TH

5 MONDAY
Moon Age Day 5   Moon Sign Canc

am...

pm...

A lift in most social matters assists you to show your best side, and t
achieve a familiar closeness in relationships that might have been missin
for a short while. Being on the same mental wavelength as colleagu
and friends is what today is all about. This can also help you to achieve
calmer state of mind.

6 TUESDAY
Moon Age Day 6   Moon Sign Le

am...

pm...

Influences regarding personal relationships could be less favourable at th
moment, and it would be best not to push such matters too hard. There
much to be said for choosing to concentrate on more casual associatio
for the time being, and for leaving major issues of love to be sorted ou
on another day.

7 WEDNESDAY
Moon Age Day 7   Moon Sign Le

am...

pm...

You have everything you need to make progress in most matters, an
what might prove most important right now is your ability to ensure tha
personal relationships are working well. Make sure that aggravation
thing of the past, and put your efforts into finding exactly the right word
to say to make those around you feel wanted and happy.

8 THURSDAY
Moon Age Day 8   Moon Sign Le

am...

pm...

If there doesn't seem to be too many emotional rewards available toda
why not concentrate on the more practical aspects of life instead? Ther
are so many possible spheres of influence for you at present that it may b
difficult to know which one you should look at first. Meanwhile, it pay
to seek the help and support you need from friends.

FRIDAY
Moon Age Day 9   Moon Sign Virgo

m...

m...

eware of relying too much on the support of colleagues or even friends
oday, as there's no guarantee that it will be there when you need it the
most. You can afford to depend on your own judgement and, if necessary,
n that of a very close friend. You are encouraged to keep work and play
ompletely separate now.

10 SATURDAY
Moon Age Day 10   Moon Sign Virgo

m...

m...

Domestic matters, which you often find tedious beyond words, could
ow seem warm, comfortable and even desirable. Maybe you have been
xpecting too much of yourself recently, and have decide that you really
o need to take refuge in what is most familiar. That's fine, though your
ove affair with the intimacies of home life could be short-lived!

11 SUNDAY
Moon Age Day 11   Moon Sign Libra

m...

m...

ttracting the kind thoughts and goodwill of others certainly should not
e difficult for you now. There is nothing at all wrong with asking for help
hen you need it, and especially if you sense that those around you are
ery willing to offer support. You may even have an opportunity to break
own specific barriers that have been in place for months or years.

LOVE	MONEY	CAREER	VITALITY

+5 +4 +3 +2 +1 −1 −2 −3 −4 −5

81

12 MONDAY
Moon Age Day 12   Moon Sign Libr

am...

pm...

This has potential be a stop-and-start sort of day, because some of wha
you want to do is a breeze, whilst other issues seem to be much mor
awkward. The general advice is to concentrate on what you can do an
not to fret over things you can't. Even a single job done well makes you
efforts worthwhile at the moment.

13 TUESDAY
Moon Age Day 13   Moon Sign Libr

am...

pm...

Trends suggest that there's something missing today, and that it may b
difficult for you to put your finger on what it is. Rather than putting a
your efforts into trying to find out, there's nothing wrong with simp
relying on your instincts. By the evening the emphasis is on your desir
for comfort and security, which is quite unusual for Gemini.

14 WEDNESDAY
Moon Age Day 14   Moon Sign Scorp

am...

pm...

Social plans may have to be re-routed, but if you are willing to thir
on your feet this needn't be too much of a problem. Under curren
influences, a planned schedule is less likely to get you where you want t
be than one that involves reacting to events. Romantically speaking, th
has potential to be a very interesting phase.

15 THURSDAY
Moon Age Day 15   Moon Sign Scorp

am...

pm...

There is great scope for attracting life's little luxuries today, somethir
that often accompanies a sense of insecurity for Gemini. It ought to b
obvious that your instincts are presently honed to perfection, and you ca
use your mixture of intuition and direct communication to gain a muc
better understanding of exactly how others operate.

16 FRIDAY
Moon Age Day 16   Moon Sign Sagittarius

m..

m..

It may well be best to keep a low profile for the next day or two while the lunar low is in residence. It isn't necessarily that you are likely to fail, merely that the quieter side of your nature is to the fore. Gemini is not the most balanced of the zodiac signs, and it does tend to veer from frenetic to frazzled. Finding a middle path is the key.

17 SATURDAY
Moon Age Day 17   Moon Sign Sagittarius

m..

m..

Rather than wasting your time on trivialities today, your best approach is to make up your mind to deal with situations one at a time. If energy seems to be in short supply, it's very important that you ration yourself. By tomorrow the planetary picture will be looking much better again, but moving mountains may well be difficult during this 24-hour period.

18 SUNDAY
Moon Age Day 18   Moon Sign Capricorn

m..

m..

The emphasis is on your desire to be yourself this weekend, and on your ability to show your best side to others. Of course you can't expect to please everyone, but that's the way life is. This would be a perfect Sunday for a change of scenery and for mixing with people who really appreciate you. Humility is not your special gift right now!

	LOVE	MONEY	CAREER	VITALITY
+5				
+4				
+3				
+2				
+1				
-1				
-2				
-3				
-4				
-5				

19 MONDAY
Moon Age Day 19   Moon Sign Capricorn

am..

pm..

The potential you have for attracting new people into your life has rarely been better than it is right now. Trends assist you to scintillate when in company, and to find the right thing to say in a range of situations. Don't be surprised if others are a little jealous of your natural ability to be at ease with the world. Carry on regardless.

20 TUESDAY
Moon Age Day 20   Moon Sign Aquarius

am..

pm..

An idea day to tackle any outstanding practical matters. You have everything you need to ensure that progress is made on specific jobs, particularly if you are willing to delegate certain tasks to others. You could charm the birds down from the trees now, and can use this talent to take your general popularity to new heights.

21 WEDNESDAY
Moon Age Day 21   Moon Sign Aquarius

am..

pm..

The very practical side of your nature is now on display. This would be a favourable time to tackle some DIY or to get to grips with the garden. The more time you have to yourself today, the better are the prospects for fun. Gemini people who have to work may have to deal with a few minor difficulties, especially after lunch.

22 THURSDAY
Moon Age Day 22   Moon Sign Pisces

am..

pm..

Once again the spotlight is now on the practicalities of life, encouraging you to keep busy from the time you get up until the time you crawl back into bed. This isn't necessarily an issue for you as it's part of the typical Gemini make-up. Confidence is very important when you have to attend any sort of meeting now.

3 FRIDAY
Moon Age Day 23   Moon Sign Pisces

....

....

ere's nothing wrong with being in a hurry to complete projects and to
ove on to whatever is next on your agenda. However, it pays to ensure
at you don't rush specific jobs, and instead, to finish one task properly
fore you embark upon the next. Routines can be quite rewarding, even
your natural instinct is to shy away from them.

4 SATURDAY
Moon Age Day 24   Moon Sign Aries

....

....

little cheek can go a long way this weekend. If there is something you
nt to do, especially a trip or maybe a shopping spree, be prepared to
t in the effort to convince others to get involved. Rather than feeling
ilty about using persuasion, simply concentrate on ensuring they are in
e right frame of mind.

5 SUNDAY
Moon Age Day 25   Moon Sign Aries

....

....

actical matters are well accented for you at the moment, though a slight
ment of disorganisation can't be ruled out. There are still gains to be
de in a financial sense, even if some of these seem to be beyond your
n ability to manipulate. Make the most of the aspects of life that are
ing your way.

				+5
				+4
				+3
				+2
				+1
LOVE	MONEY	CAREER	VITALITY	
				-1
				-2
				-3
				-4
				-5

26 MONDAY
Moon Age Day 26   Moon Sign Tau

am...

pm...

The potential you have for attracting just the right sort of people i
your life has rarely been better than it seems to be right now. Confiden
boosting exercises are important, and you need to be prepared to t
advantage of them whether or not you are actively seeking them. T
could be a fine time to step up the temperature in a romantic attachme

27 TUESDAY
Moon Age Day 27   Moon Sign Tau

am...

pm...

You can't expect everyone to listen to what you are saying, even if you
certain in your own mind that you are speaking common sense. Perh
it's time to try a different approach, particularly when you are deal
with loved ones. Committing yourself to finding new solutions to
problems is part of what present trends are about.

28 WEDNESDAY
Moon Age Day 28   Moon Sign Tau

am...

pm...

There are gains to be made from contacts with people who either liv
a distance or have not spoken to you for a while. In a personal sense
would be an excellent time to bury a hatchet, and this gives you a cha
to show the diplomatic side of Gemini. You might even be able to h
rifts that have nothing to do with you.

29 THURSDAY
Moon Age Day 0   Moon Sign Gem

am...

pm...

Don't be afraid to gamble a little, particularly if you are very sure that
risk of failure is small. You can afford to push yourself quite hard now,
this encourages a very positive frame of mind, which is really all it take
ensure success. Your mind is working like lightning, especially in term
solving any sort of puzzle.

0 FRIDAY *Moon Age Day 1   Moon Sign Gemini*

....

....

though you are still very much on a roll you might have to stop yourself
your tracks on one or two occasions today in order to let others catch
. Although this can be somewhat frustrating you still manage to forge
ead all the same. Confidence boosting exercises come along all the time.

1 SATURDAY *Moon Age Day 2   Moon Sign Cancer*

....

....

e focus is now on your ability to persuade relatives and friends alike to
t themselves out in order to accommodate your wishes. The desire to
ep up appearances is also highlighted for Gemini at the moment. That's
 very well, but if you go too far in this direction you could appear
mpous.

SUNDAY *Moon Age Day 3   Moon Sign Cancer*

....

....

e start of a new month is noteworthy in this case because it heralds a
ing love on your part for anything odd, unusual or downright peculiar.
u might decide to delve into the past for some reason, and this can
er you the chance to turn over stones wherever you go. Curiosity is
e, so just get on with it!

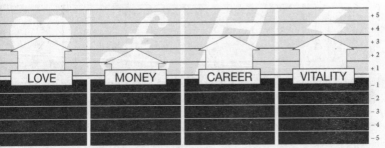

June

2014

YOUR MONTH AT A GLANCE

+ = Opportunities are around ● = Be on the defensive   = Life is pretty ordina

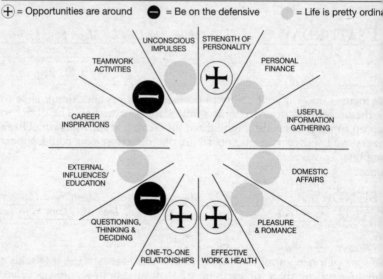

- UNCONSCIOUS IMPULSES
- STRENGTH OF PERSONALITY
- TEAMWORK ACTIVITIES
- PERSONAL FINANCE
- CAREER INSPIRATIONS
- USEFUL INFORMATION GATHERING
- EXTERNAL INFLUENCES/ EDUCATION
- DOMESTIC AFFAIRS
- QUESTIONING, THINKING & DECIDING
- PLEASURE & ROMANCE
- ONE-TO-ONE RELATIONSHIPS
- EFFECTIVE WORK & HEALTH

JUNE HIGHS AND LOWS

Here I show you how the rhythms of the Moon will affect you this mont Like the tide, your energies and abilities will rise and fall with its patter When it is above the centre line, go for it, when it is below, you shou be resting.

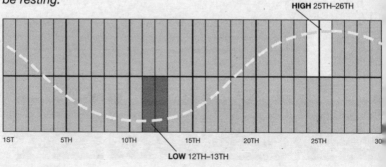

HIGH 25TH–26TH

1ST   5TH   10TH   15TH   20TH   25TH   30

LOW 12TH–13TH

MONDAY
Moon Age Day 4   Moon Sign Cancer

n...

n...

ight tensions are possible within specific relationships, particularly later
the day. Whether or not you are contributing to this state of affairs,
nly you can decide, and it's something that's worth thinking about
arefully. Be ready to deal with new tasks at work today, which could well
ome along just when you think you are on top of things!

TUESDAY
Moon Age Day 5   Moon Sign Leo

n...

n...

ight now the focus is firmly on your ability to tackle practical issues, so
ou may decide that the theoretical side of life can take something of a
ack seat. That's fine, though planning still counts for a great deal, and
hould help you to avoid doing the same thing more than once. A few
inutes' contemplation can save hours now.

WEDNESDAY
Moon Age Day 6   Moon Sign Leo

n...

m...

his could be a time of some financial progress if you handle things
roperly. Trends assist you to get plenty done in a practical sense, and this
akes it less likely that you will have to repeat yourself. There are strong
ncentives available for you to make significant changes in and around
our home, though you may well need some help.

THURSDAY
Moon Age Day 7   Moon Sign Virgo

n...

m...

ou are encouraged to make today as warm and cosy as you can, especially
you have been dealing with the somewhat stark realities of life in recent
mes. The family-minded aspect of Gemini is emphasised, encouraging
ou to spend plenty of time at home. Don't be afraid to show the
ntimental side of your nature.

6 FRIDAY
Moon Age Day 8   Moon Sign Virg

am...

pm...

If feelings are running high among friends, the last thing you need is t
find yourself the filling in a sandwich between two opposing factions
Avoid taking sides if at all possible, though in the end you may decid
you have no option but to do so. Your best tact and diplomacy can mak
all the difference now.

7 SATURDAY   ☿
Moon Age Day 9   Moon Sign Virg

am...

pm...

Trends bring an interlude in which you may feel less in control of you
affairs than you would wish, though you needn't allow this to have a
adverse bearing on what you achieve this weekend. This is not a time fo
striding forward in a professional or practical sense, but rather, one i
which it pays to watch and wait. Social activities are well accented.

8 SUNDAY   ☿
Moon Age Day 10   Moon Sign Libr

am...

pm...

There are gains to be made today by those of you who work at a weekend
though the very best potential relates to Gemini people who can call thi
Sunday their own. With some almost magical influences playing aroun
you at present, you have what it takes to make a great impression o
others, and to create an excellent day for yourself.

	LOVE		MONEY		CAREER		VITALITY

MONDAY ☿ *Moon Age Day 11 Moon Sign Libra*

n...

n...

here is no reason to hang back at the beginning of this week and it is
nportant that you take advantage of opportunities as and when they
ise. However, it may be more difficult to show quite as much patience
s has been the case recently, which is one of the reasons why it would be
nsible to listen to what someone slightly less mercurial has to say.

0 TUESDAY ☿ *Moon Age Day 12 Moon Sign Scorpio*

n...

m...

our powers of communication are to the fore, assisting you to curb any
ndency you may have to speak out without thinking. Lo and behold,
ou have plenty of scope to increase your popularity yet again, and to
ake a strong impression on the world at large. You can afford to make
is a very busy sort of day.

1 WEDNESDAY ☿ *Moon Age Day 13 Moon Sign Scorpio*

n...

m...

laterial affairs have a great deal to offer you, and this would be an ideal
me to build upon recent fresh starts you have made. You need to achieve
balance between finding time to think and having hours during which
ou can choose to enjoy yourself. Getting together with pals could be
n, especially ones you don't see too often.

2 THURSDAY ☿ *Moon Age Day 14 Moon Sign Sagittarius*

n...

m...

ou would be wise not to take on too many commitments today. The
nar low is around, and does nothing to boost your strength. Your best
pproach is to concentrate on things you enjoy and, if possible, take a
otal break from responsibilities. You can't expect everyone to agree with
our ideas at the moment, and patience is the key.

13 FRIDAY ☿ *Moon Age Day 15   Moon Sign Sagittari*

am...

pm...

The lunar low has potential to take the wind out of your sails but is on
really noticeable if you have to work hard today. Otherwise, there is muc
to be said for taking a break from routine and enjoying what life offe
simply and without demand. Even if confidence takes a dent, the pha
won't last long.

14 SATURDAY ☿ *Moon Age Day 16   Moon Sign Capricor*

am...

pm...

This would be an ideal time to focus on any intimate problems th
exist, but without allowing them to get you down. Although the lun
low is now finished, it could take you a day or so to regain some of th
momentum you had before. If you need some help and support, why n
ask friends to lend a hand?

15 SUNDAY ☿ *Moon Age Day 17   Moon Sign Capricor*

am...

pm...

In financial terms you have scope to make some positive progress generall
though some of this could rely on you capitalising on good luck rath
than good planning. If you have been looking forward to a trip, it mig
be good to look at all the details and to make certain you have dealt wi
every potential. Beware of being strung along in a personal situation.

	LOVE	MONEY	CAREER	VITALITY
5 +				
4+				
3+				
2+				
1 +				
1 -				
2 -				
3 -				
4 -				
5 -				

6 MONDAY ☿ *Moon Age Day 18   Moon Sign Aquarius*

n..

n..

you need to be very aware of who you are willing to trust right now. This doesn't refer to friends you have known for a long time, but to the odd individual who might try to pull the wool over your eyes. Your intuition counts for a great deal under current planetary influences, and can be your best guide at present.

7 TUESDAY ☿ *Moon Age Day 19   Moon Sign Aquarius*

n..

n..

Make sure your winning ways are once again on display and that you blow away any difficulties you were facing on a fresh breeze of optimism. The great thing about being a Gemini is that very little bothers you for long at a time. Financial trends are encouraging, and you might even be able to get the better of a former adversary.

8 WEDNESDAY ☿ *Moon Age Day 20   Moon Sign Pisces*

n..

n..

It's important to take advantage of all the encouragement that is available today, which comes just at the time you need it the most. If you can persuade people to be on your side, this should help you to feel more comfortable with life in general. The diplomatic side of Gemini is quite clearly on display at this stage of the week.

9 THURSDAY ☿ *Moon Age Day 21   Moon Sign Pisces*

n..

n..

When it comes to the practical side of life, trends suggest that you know exactly what to do. However, you ought to be prepared to deal with some slight complications in romantic situations. Emotionally speaking, this isn't the most favourable interlude ever. Bear this in mind, and try to avoid taking offence at things that aren't intended to be in the least insulting.

20 FRIDAY ☿ *Moon Age Day 22 Moon Sign Ar*

am..

pm..

A period of emotional intensity is indicated for Gemini at this time, an the fact that this coincides with the end of a working week might lead to few problems. Does it appear that others are doing everything they can upset your plans? You need to ask yourself whether you are really seei things quite as positively as would normally be the case.

21 SATURDAY ☿ *Moon Age Day 23 Moon Sign Ar*

am..

pm..

Once again, you may feel that your usual way of working is bei challenged by others, but it's possible that you are not being quite as cle in your thinking as would normally be the case. Your best way forwa is to avoid judgements of either people or situations, and in some cas make a determined effort to suspend belief for a while.

22 SUNDAY ☿ *Moon Age Day 24 Moon Sign Ar*

am..

pm..

By all means think about self-improvement, though recognise that makir progress in any concrete sense might be a few months down the line, focus on planning and deciding how to approach situations. Be willing allow those you care for deeply to play a more significant role in areas your life in which they aren't usually involved.

	LOVE	MONEY	CAREER	VITALITY

3 MONDAY ☿ *Moon Age Day 25 Moon Sign Taurus*

n..

n..

here is much to be said for taking full advantage of any invitations that e on offer around now. Even if it means doing something you are not o keen on, the result could be much more enjoyable than you think. verall, there is plenty of stimulation and happiness to be found today, rticularly in the company of friends.

4 TUESDAY ☿ *Moon Age Day 26 Moon Sign Taurus*

n..

m..

here is potential for personal relationships to try your patience a little day, and some extra effort is needed in order to avoid losing your mper over issues that are really not important. Be prepared to respond the strong opinions of others about issues that are specifically your usiness. Patience and diplomacy can work wonders!

5 WEDNESDAY ☿ *Moon Age Day 27 Moon Sign Gemini*

n..

m..

he opportunity to forge ahead with new and interesting ideas comes ow, as the lunar high offers some of the best incentives of the month. his is no time to be held back, but a period during which you can afford push the bounds of possibility as far and as fast as you are able. Travel well starred.

6 THURSDAY ☿ *Moon Age Day 28 Moon Sign Gemini*

m..

m..

Once again your foot should be on the gas pedal and you have everything ou need to move forward very positively. Even if professional progress n't easy at this stage of the week, remember that the lunar high offers ll sorts of other incentives. Make the most of these and push ahead on as any fronts as you can.

27 FRIDAY ☿ *Moon Age Day 0   Moon Sign Canc*

am ....

pm...

Trying to achieve some strong internal changes within yourself is fir
though productive progress should also be possible today. What mig
become an issue is if you realise that some of what you are doing gc
against the grain. Expressing yourself isn't difficult, so maybe this is t
time to have an honest chat with someone.

28 SATURDAY ☿ *Moon Age Day 1   Moon Sign Canc*

am ....

pm...

There may be no quick solutions to life's little problems, though if you a
willing to seek the advice of an expert you could probably save yours
a lot of hard work. Sometimes it's difficult for Gemini to eat humble p
and to admit that others might have some of the answers. Go on! I
good for your soul.

29 SUNDAY ☿ *Moon Age Day 2   Moon Sign Canc*

am ....

pm...

A more freewheeling attitude to life can work wonders at the mome
and let's face it – that's your natural way. Trends assist you to use yo
persuasive powers, and there should be very little beyond your capabiliti
if you set your mind to it. Even casual conversations can enable you
reap rewards later in the day.

	LOVE	MONEY	CAREER	VITALITY
5 +				
4+				
3+				
2+				
1 +				
1 -				
2 -				
3 -				
4 -				
5 -				

0 MONDAY   ☿   *Moon Age Day 3   Moon Sign Leo*

....

....

ncentration is the order of the day, and should assist you to dig deep
order to get to the root of a specific situation right now. However,
hough you have what it takes to keep moving forward positively, there
: signs that focusing on individual issues could still be a challenge.
rtainties are few at the moment.

TUESDAY   ☿   *Moon Age Day 4   Moon Sign Leo*

....

....

nat you need most at the moment is a release from routine and the
ance to do more or less whatever takes your fancy. Avoid getting
volved in discussions or arguments that can't further your objectives at
and where it is possible you need to play the honest broker amongst
agreeing friends.

WEDNESDAY   *Moon Age Day 5   Moon Sign Virgo*

....

....

ready to deal with any ups and downs you encounter today, particularly
terms of relationships. Although you have what it takes to get on the
ght side of most people, there are always going to be exceptions. It's
tural for rules and regulations to get on your nerves around this time.
ur best response is to shrug your shoulders and smile.

THURSDAY   *Moon Age Day 6   Moon Sign Virgo*

....

....

day works best if you can keep on the move and work hard to get
ings going your way. There isn't much mileage in staying in the same
ace, and travel of any sort is supported by a number of present trends.
sporting activities it pays to go for gold, though it has to be said that
u might only manage silver.

4 FRIDAY
Moon Age Day 7   Moon Sign Vi

am ....

pm..

Activities that are taking place out there in the wider world could
hold more appeal than home-based matters today. That's fine, as l
as you don't appear to be deliberately ignoring your nearest and dear
Gemini is a creature of the moment, and others probably realise this f
However, a little consideration can go a long way.

5 SATURDAY
Moon Age Day 8   Moon Sign Li

am ....

pm..

Current influences make this an ideal interlude for making finan
progress, though it's important to act fast because the Sun only rema
in your solar second house until just after the 20th. If there are any d
to be done, this would be the perfect time to do them. Understand
the way those around you are thinking shouldn't be hard today.

6 SUNDAY
Moon Age Day 9   Moon Sign Li

am ....

pm..

All aspects of communication are highlighted at present, even if t
don't seem important at the time. The most casual comment can o
pause for thought, and might assist you to achieve something stupend
in the fullness of time. The chatty side of your nature, combined w
your ability to listen carefully too, gives you the best of both worlds.

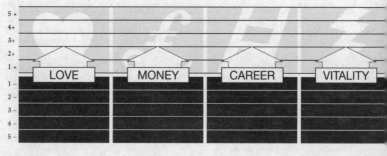

July

2014

ΙR Month at a Glance

= Opportunities are around   ● = Be on the defensive   ● = Life is pretty ordinary

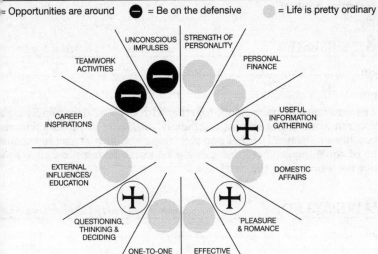

TEAMWORK ACTIVITIES

UNCONSCIOUS IMPULSES

STRENGTH OF PERSONALITY

PERSONAL FINANCE

CAREER INSPIRATIONS

USEFUL INFORMATION GATHERING

EXTERNAL INFLUENCES/ EDUCATION

DOMESTIC AFFAIRS

QUESTIONING, THINKING & DECIDING

PLEASURE & ROMANCE

ONE-TO-ONE RELATIONSHIPS

EFFECTIVE WORK & HEALTH

Y Highs and Lows

re I show you how the rhythms of the Moon will affect you this month.
e the tide, your energies and abilities will rise and fall with its pattern.
en it is above the centre line, go for it, when it is below, you should
resting.

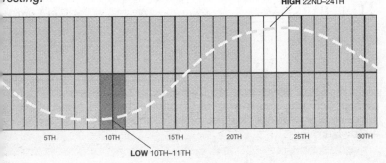

HIGH 22ND–24TH

5TH   10TH   15TH   20TH   25TH   30TH

LOW 10TH–11TH

7 MONDAY
Moon Age Day 10   Moon Sign Scor

am..

pm..

Be prepared to welcome old faces back into your life. The present posit of the Moon assists you to gain a great deal from meetings with th from the past, and such encounters can have some sort of positive bear on your immediate future. There is much about today that could be s as odd or unusual.

8 TUESDAY
Moon Age Day 11   Moon Sign Scor

am..

pm..

The art of good conversation, together with the attendant popularity t you can achieve as a result, is definitely your forte at present. Howe you need to remember that not everything you hear at the moment be of equal importance, and it might be worth taking some time to out the wheat from the chaff.

9 WEDNESDAY
Moon Age Day 12   Moon Sign Scor

am..

pm..

As far as personal and emotional security are concerned, this would be excellent time to make sure you are looking after yourself. For the time in days you have a chance to sit and take stock, and shouldn't b too much of a rush to get things done. It might even appear that so problems are solving themselves today!

10 THURSDAY
Moon Age Day 13   Moon Sign Sagitta

am..

pm..

With the Moon in your opposite zodiac sign you may not be able make masses of progress today. If settling for second-best doesn't app perhaps deferring the effort would be more sensible? Instead of taking anything new, why not clear the decks for actions you know are necess a little later?

1 FRIDAY *Moon Age Day 14   Moon Sign Sagittarius*

....

....

is is a time which is ideal for actively choosing to sit back and take
ck of situations, if only because the continuing lunar low does nothing
encourage direct intervention or movement. Prior planning is always
ood thing, though it isn't something Gemini people take into account
ough. You can do so now.

2 SATURDAY *Moon Age Day 15   Moon Sign Capricorn*

....

....

terms of getting along with others, what may have seemed so easy a
days ago could well be more difficult now. Making it clear you are
willing to make definite compromises is all very well, though this fact
ne can get you into some hot water. Arriving at conclusions that don't
lly make sense is also another potential difficulty.

3 SUNDAY *Moon Age Day 16   Moon Sign Capricorn*

....

....

ends suggest that you are not backward at coming forward at the
oment, which is going to stand you in good stead socially. You need to
ar in mind that not everything you have to say is of interest to everyone
u meet, and it is important to know when you are over-egging the
dding. Balance is required.

| LOVE | MONEY | CAREER | VITALITY |

+5 +4 +3 +2 +1 -1 -2 -3 -4 -5

14 MONDAY

Moon Age Day 17   Moon Sign Aquar

am ....

pm ....

Circumstances are improving for dealing with money matters. You hav
good head on your shoulders at the beginning of this week, and can
this interlude to make a favourable impression on those who have pov
and influence. In your personal life, be on the look-out for any awkw
types who are about.

15 TUESDAY

Moon Age Day 18   Moon Sign Aquar

am ....

pm ....

Casual conversations sometimes don't get you anywhere, though if y
make the most of them today, you can ensure that they do. Keep yo
ears open because the truth of many situations lies just below the surfa
Routines can also be something of a bind, particularly if they don't le
you the amount of time you feel you need to get on with other import
matters which are occupying your thoughts.

16 WEDNESDAY

Moon Age Day 19   Moon Sign Pi.

am ....

pm ....

Today offers you scope to make progress in terms of your perso
attachments, though your interactions with superiors or colleagues mig
not be quite as favourable. This is a traditional period for holidays, an
you're a Gemini who has chosen this time to take a break, it's up to y
to make full use of all the potential on offer.

17 THURSDAY

Moon Age Day 20   Moon Sign Pi.

am ....

pm ....

If you keep your current objectives sensible, the gains you can ma
should be in direct proportion to the amount of effort you are willing
put in. Getting others to keep up with you might be the only real probl
at the moment. There are occasions when you can't, in which case y
need to carry on regardless!

FRIDAY   *Moon Age Day 21   Moon Sign Aries*

....

....

fessional dealings are well accented, and you have what it takes to start
ing the rewards of any new responsibilities you have recently taken
Romance can offer you a haven to which you can retreat once the
rt of the day is over. Trends indicate a strong see-saw effect in your
now, between your hard edge and your soft centre.

SATURDAY   *Moon Age Day 22   Moon Sign Aries*

....

....

ur ability to come up with some excellent ideas is now emphasised, and
only slight frustration is that you can't put them all into practice at
same time. Even Gemini can only do so many things at once, though
re's nothing to stop you from offering advice to others and assisting
m to make a brand new start.

SUNDAY   *Moon Age Day 23   Moon Sign Taurus*

....

....

ere are influences around at the moment that can be used to inspire
eresting and rewarding conversations. Gemini is never at the back of
class when it comes to talking, but you can afford to be even more
nmunicative at the moment than would normally be the case. Don't
too quick to take offence over a casual remark.

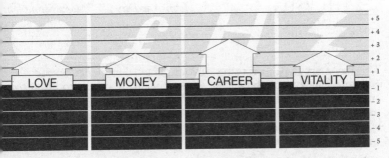

103

21 MONDAY
Moon Age Day 24   Moon Sign Tau

am ....

pm...

It is possible that you could get ahead at work this week partly as a resul
your own efforts, but also because you are able to capitalise on some v
useful information. It's time to show that you are active and enterprisi
and that you have the ability to think on your feet. But there's noth
new about that for the sign of Gemini!

22 TUESDAY
Moon Age Day 25   Moon Sign Gem

am ....

pm...

All of a sudden you have an opportunity to increase the pace of
markedly, and to take advantage of increased amounts of general luck. T
lunar high offers new incentives, though some of these will be perso
rather than professional. Socially speaking there are definite gains to
made from putting yourself in the limelight now.

23 WEDNESDAY
Moon Age Day 26   Moon Sign Gem

am ....

pm...

The lunar high gives you a chance to improve your financial wherewith
and to make some fairly straightforward speculations, particularly if y
apply some clear-thinking to the issue. It's also possible to find out h
important you are to those around you, and this could be a welco
boost to your ego. Be ready to lend others a hand, particularly relative

24 THURSDAY
Moon Age Day 27   Moon Sign Gem

am ....

pm...

This day marks a peak in terms of your personal influence on the worl
large. You have everything you need to persuade others to listen to y
and for this reason alone it pays to share all those ideas you have be
harbouring for so long. It's time to show that you are active, inspiri
magnetic and a must to know.

25 FRIDAY
Moon Age Day 28   Moon Sign Cancer

am ....

pm..

There is a strong tendency towards developing new methods of working, combined with a desire to get to your goals by simply bulldozing your way through. How successful this turns out to be remains to be seen, but you do have everything necessary to get on well with others in a personal or a romantic sense.

26 SATURDAY
Moon Age Day 29   Moon Sign Cancer

am ....

pm..

Friendships can be both stimulating and frustrating – and at one and the same time! Much of this depends on whether pals are pulling their weight, and whether you are having to respond to their unreasonable demands. It's worth seeking out those who might be able to make your life easier and whose natural warmth comes as a very definite tonic.

27 SUNDAY
Moon Age Day 0   Moon Sign Leo

am ....

pm..

There are new and exciting prospects on offer, but they won't come and find you. Search the world today in order to find what you specifically want, and don't take no for an answer when it comes to any issue that you see as being very important. With a limited budget right now, keeping an eye on what you spend is essential.

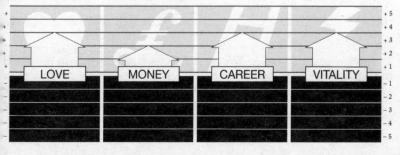

28 MONDAY
Moon Age Day 1   Moon Sign Leo

am ....

pm ....

Be prepared to put your career plans into action. In those areas of life where you have planned carefully, now is the time to take the bull by the horns. You can persuade others to give you support when you need it the most, and there is much to be said for getting more involved with specific local issues.

29 TUESDAY
Moon Age Day 2   Moon Sign Leo

am ....

pm ....

Stop and think before you forge ahead with anything especially financial commitments. Do you really want to spend money right now? Is it necessary to have more than you really need? There are good reasons to ask such questions now, and the answers might well surprise you. You may decide that in many ways, simple is best today.

30 WEDNESDAY
Moon Age Day 3   Moon Sign Virgo

am ....

pm ....

You are entering a period that could best be described as 'adequate' particularly in terms of your opportunities for progress at work. Nevertheless, there is a certain restless streak in evidence, and the best way to counter this is to make a number of subtle changes. This would be another favourable time for any sort of travel.

31 THURSDAY
Moon Age Day 4   Moon Sign Virgo

am ....

pm ....

Trends suggest a slightly selfish quality to your nature right now, though this is probably born out of necessity rather than any real desire to look after number one. You might decide at the end of the day that only by feathering your own nest will you be in a position to offer the sort of assistance to others you would wish.

1 FRIDAY
Moon Age Day 5   Moon Sign Libra

am...

pm...

Today is about building on promising starts as far as your plans are concerned and looking around for the sort of support that could prove to be invaluable. Meanwhile, you have scope to discover that romance is a key point of the day, together with the opportunity to attract some unexpected compliments.

2 SATURDAY
Moon Age Day 6   Moon Sign Libra

am...

pm...

Even if you feel you should be doing a dozen different things at once right now, in the end you might have to settle for two or three. Gemini is versatile, though not superhuman, and you need to remember that less done well is better than more done badly. This is self-evident – though not always to Gemini!

3 SUNDAY
Moon Age Day 7   Moon Sign Libra

am...

pm...

There is an emphasis on your extrovert qualities this Sunday, but of course there isn't anything too surprising about that. However, in some ways you can use today to make up for lost time, particularly if you haven't been satisfied with some of your recent progress. Time spent with family and friends counts for a great deal now.

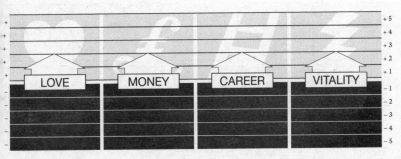

Ⅱ

August

2014

YOUR MONTH AT A GLANCE

$\oplus$ = Opportunities are around $\ominus$ = Be on the defensive   ● = Life is pretty ordina

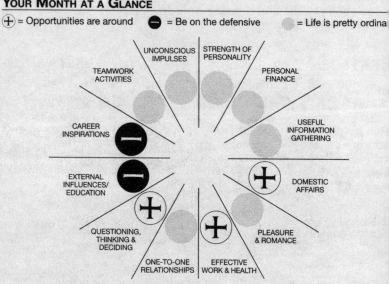

- UNCONSCIOUS IMPULSES
- STRENGTH OF PERSONALITY
- TEAMWORK ACTIVITIES
- PERSONAL FINANCE
- CAREER INSPIRATIONS
- USEFUL INFORMATION GATHERING
- EXTERNAL INFLUENCES/ EDUCATION
- DOMESTIC AFFAIRS
- QUESTIONING, THINKING & DECIDING
- PLEASURE & ROMANCE
- ONE-TO-ONE RELATIONSHIPS
- EFFECTIVE WORK & HEALTH

AUGUST HIGHS AND LOWS

Here I show you how the rhythms of the Moon will affect you this month Like the tide, your energies and abilities will rise and fall with its patterr When it is above the centre line, go for it, when it is below, you shoul be resting.

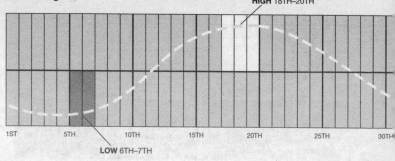

HIGH 18TH–20TH

1ST   5TH   10TH   15TH   20TH   25TH   30TH

LOW 6TH–7TH

MONDAY   *Moon Age Day 8   Moon Sign Scorpio*

n..

n..

ur knack of getting information out of people is second to none at esent, so don't hold back when it comes to gently interrogating others. his can be especially useful at work and if you are a Gemini who is esently between jobs, this might be a particularly good time to keep ur eyes open.

TUESDAY   *Moon Age Day 9   Moon Sign Scorpio*

n..

n..

u can gain a great deal from your domestic circumstances and rroundings at this stage of the month, even if you don't have as much me as you would wish to spend with your family. The spotlight is also n travel at the moment, making this an excellent time for Gemini to take y sort of break.

WEDNESDAY   *Moon Age Day 10   Moon Sign Sagittarius*

n..

m..

ow and steady wins almost any race today. Trying to barge your way rough is not to be recommended, and a measured approach definitely orks best during the lunar low. At this stage of the month, there's othing wrong with relying on the help and support you can elicit from thers, so why not lean on friends in some way?

THURSDAY   *Moon Age Day 11   Moon Sign Sagittarius*

n..

m..

s the lunar low continues, a few disappointments are possible today, though these are not necessarily of any real consequence. Once gain, the advice is to stick to simple things and avoid any unnecessary mplications. An ideal interlude for seeking out friends you don't see ery often, or spending time at home with family members.

8 FRIDAY
Moon Age Day 12   Moon Sign Capricor

am...

pm...

Today's trends encourage a busy and active approach. This can act as a antidote to the last couple of days and enables you to realise that yo haven't lost anything as a result of the less fortunate period. Don't be to quick to jump to conclusions with regard to your personal life, and avo jealousy like the plague.

9 SATURDAY
Moon Age Day 13   Moon Sign Capricor

am...

pm...

A period of domestic reward is indicated for the weekend. Although yo might have thought that this would be a good time to be on the mov in the end you need to ask whether hearth and home have more to off you. You can afford to leave a few jobs until later, or else look around fc someone else to do them for you.

10 SUNDAY
Moon Age Day 14   Moon Sign Aquari

am...

pm...

It's important to capitalise on new and important information you ca discover now, perhaps coming from the direction of a friend or associat It is worth paying attention today, and being ready to act on specif situations as soon as possible. Make the most of the favourable romant prospects that also have a part to play in today's opportunities.

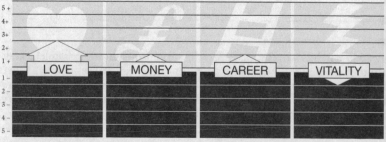

1 MONDAY
Moon Age Day 15   Moon Sign Aquarius

m..

m..

There is scope for you to broaden your personal horizons around now, and present trends also assist your efforts to create some excitement. Acting on impulse can often be risky, but if you use your Gemini instincts to the full you might even be able to get away with things that others can only dream about.

2 TUESDAY
Moon Age Day 16   Moon Sign Pisces

m..

m..

In a social sense you are encouraged to branch out in some way at this stage of the week. Those of you who have been paying attention might have noticed that professional trends are not so obvious around now. For this reason alone, there is much to be said for choosing this period in which to take a holiday.

3 WEDNESDAY
Moon Age Day 17   Moon Sign Pisces

m..

m..

There are signs that concentrating on whatever you think you do best is probably the best response to present trends. What might not be so sensible would be to start too many new projects. Remember that there are only so many hours in a day, and the number doesn't increase just because you are a Gemini!

4 THURSDAY
Moon Age Day 18   Moon Sign Aries

m..

m..

The pull of the past can be especially strong around this time. Certain forms of communication could prompt you to focus more on situations that you thought were long gone. You need to be very positive about the present too, and should not allow yourself to become too absorbed by your nostalgic frame of mind.

15 FRIDAY

Moon Age Day 19   Moon Sign Ar

am...

pm...

Matters of the heart are at their most fulfilling, assisting you to create
warm and happy evening after what is potentially a fairly steady sort
day. Planning for the weekend is the order of the day. The ideal scenar
would be to have a day or two out, possibly doing something you see
an exciting break from the norm.

16 SATURDAY

Moon Age Day 20   Moon Sign Taur

am...

pm...

Productivity remains emphasised, but you need to bear in mind that yo
have at least a couple of quieter days in front of you and there is a stror
need to consolidate some of your efforts. Even casual conversations ca
allow you to gather some good ideas for actions in the future, but there
nothing wrong with keeping at least some plans on ice.

17 SUNDAY

Moon Age Day 21   Moon Sign Taur

am...

pm...

This is not a day during which you should be taking too many chance
On the contrary, it's a question of sticking to tried and tested paths ar
seeking sound advice from those you trust. There's also an emphasis o
communication, making this an ideal time to get in touch with peop
you don't see too often.

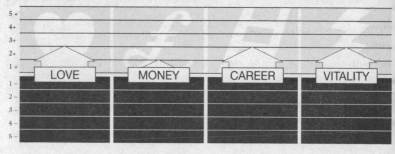

8 MONDAY
Moon Age Day 22   Moon Sign Gemini

....

....

ep up the good work as the lunar high arrives, and be willing to enjoy urself on this summer Monday. With the ability to attract positive sponses from almost every direction, getting your own way ought to be ild's play. Romantic opportunities abound, and in terms of finding the ht words you have what it takes to be a veritable poet now.

9 TUESDAY
Moon Age Day 23   Moon Sign Gemini

....

....

e lunar high continues, assisting you to come up with some particularly eresting ways in which you can get ahead. You can be quite certain your actions today, and more than happy to push your luck in the owledge that you have what it takes to follow through. Today can be antidote to what has been a sometimes quiet period.

0 WEDNESDAY
Moon Age Day 24   Moon Sign Gemini

....

....

ep your foot well and truly on the gas pedal and make the most of the sitive influences that are around at the moment. This is a favourable ne to let professional matters take centre stage, particularly if you've pt them on the back burner for a while. Seeing what you want for the ture shouldn't be difficult now.

1 THURSDAY
Moon Age Day 25   Moon Sign Cancer

....

....

u benefit most today from those associations closest to home. As you ter a temporary but important thoughtful phase, the degree of success u can register out there in the wider world is not so great, whereas you ve scope to feel secure, happy and content when in your own abode. Be the look-out for important communications later.

22 FRIDAY

Moon Age Day 26   Moon Sign Can.

am ....

pm ....

The indications are that you can find most happiness today in situatic
where you can use that great Gemini initiative. However, beware of taki
anything for granted. It's worth being careful around others, particula
those you see as rivals or opponents. You need to be ready to respon
any slight problems do arise.

23 SATURDAY

Moon Age Day 27   Moon Sign I

am ....

pm ....

The real Gemini flair for discussions is emphasised at the moment, than
to the present position of the Sun in your solar chart. Wide-rangi
conversations are the order of the day, and you may decide there
virtually nothing you are unwilling to talk about. This can certainly h
you to make a good impression when it matters the most.

24 SUNDAY

Moon Age Day 28   Moon Sign I

am ....

pm ....

Your natural desire to be close to others is much highlighted at t
moment, and this gives you everything you need for an especially wa
and happy interlude on the romantic front. Financial matters are w
accented, and while this doesn't necessarily mean you will be rolling
cash at present, you might find you are better off than you thought.

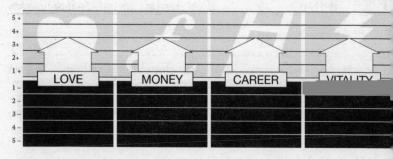

5 MONDAY   *Moon Age Day 0   Moon Sign Leo*

m...

m...

he time is right to enjoy the benefits that come from a greater sense
' personal freedom – something that is always of great importance to
emini. Don't allow yourself to be held back by any slight irritations,
ıt push forward all the same. The more cheerful you remain, the more
:ople you can get to notice you.

6 TUESDAY   *Moon Age Day 1   Moon Sign Virgo*

m...

m...

erhaps you need to be more aware of the over-confidence of those you
)unt as competitors. You don't necessarily need to react at all strongly to
is, but you can certainly make use of it. Simply remain cool, calm and
)llected, and show the whole world that you know what you are talking
)out and what you are doing.

7 WEDNESDAY   *Moon Age Day 2   Moon Sign Virgo*

m...

m...

here are now benefits to be had from expansive social matters, and the
1ore you put yourself about, the more you have potential to achieve.
ven if you are taking the same approach at the very start of the day as
)u were yesterday, this is a state of affairs that can be changed extremely
uickly, in favour of a go-getting you!

8 THURSDAY   *Moon Age Day 3   Moon Sign Libra*

m...

m...

etter co-operation and compromise can make all the difference at work
nder today's influences, and it's also worth putting some extra effort
ito any sort of educational pursuit in which you are involved. Why not
hlist the support of someone you know to be very knowledgeable? Don't
)rget to give credit where credit's due.

29 FRIDAY

Moon Age Day 4   Moon Sign Lib.

am..

pm..

Changing your plans regarding a short trip might actually offer positi
opportunities. As is your usual way, try to remain flexible and don't ma
too many hard and fast arrangements that cannot be altered if necessa
An entertaining period socially is possible from simply being in the rig
place at the best time.

30 SATURDAY

Moon Age Day 5   Moon Sign Lib.

am..

pm..

Attending to several different tasks at the same time should be no proble
to you at the moment, and gives you a chance to relish the cut and thru
of a busy life. Is it tricky for you to get going with things you have be
ignoring for a while? It's up to you to ensure that the new starts you ma
are positive ones.

31 SUNDAY

Moon Age Day 6   Moon Sign Scorp

am..

pm..

A continued boost to all matters professional is there for the takin
though of course this trend may not be very useful if you are relaxii
during Sunday. It's worth getting out and about, even if you don't g
very far. You really will benefit from some fresh air and you need ext
stimulus if possible.

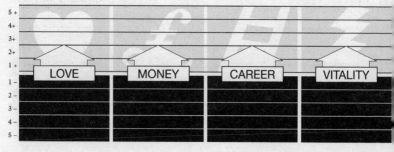

September 2014

YOUR MONTH AT A GLANCE

= Opportunities are around   = Be on the defensive   = Life is pretty ordinary

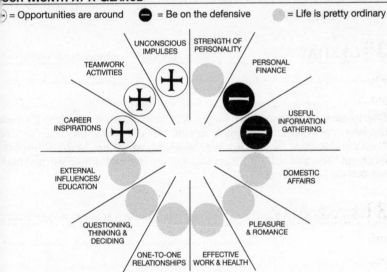

- UNCONSCIOUS IMPULSES
- STRENGTH OF PERSONALITY
- TEAMWORK ACTIVITIES
- PERSONAL FINANCE
- CAREER INSPIRATIONS
- USEFUL INFORMATION GATHERING
- EXTERNAL INFLUENCES/ EDUCATION
- DOMESTIC AFFAIRS
- QUESTIONING, THINKING & DECIDING
- PLEASURE & ROMANCE
- ONE-TO-ONE RELATIONSHIPS
- EFFECTIVE WORK & HEALTH

SEPTEMBER HIGHS AND LOWS

Here I show you how the rhythms of the Moon will affect you this month. Like the tide, your energies and abilities will rise and fall with its pattern. When it is above the centre line, go for it, when it is below, you should be resting.

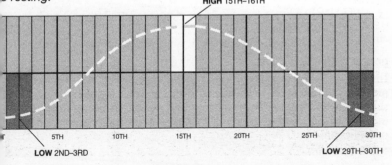

HIGH 15TH–16TH

LOW 2ND–3RD

LOW 29TH–30TH

5TH   10TH   15TH   20TH   25TH   30TH

1 MONDAY
Moon Age Day 7   Moon Sign Scorpio

am ....

pm...

This is a time to let go socially and be willing to go with the flow. Part of this is persuading those around you to make some of the arrangements, while you simply fall in with their plans. Of course, you can still find ways to be centre stage because that's the sort of person you are. In any case, it's expected of you.

2 TUESDAY
Moon Age Day 8   Moon Sign Sagittarius

am ....

pm...

Energy may now be in short supply with the arrival of the lunar low, and the best way to deal with this is to ride out the storm for a day or two. Today is not ideal for making big decisions, which are best left until the weekend. You can still find ways to have fun, though much of this might depend on other people.

3 WEDNESDAY
Moon Age Day 9   Moon Sign Sagittarius

am ....

pm...

There is now a fairly benign focus on domestic and family issues. You shouldn't have to go too far from home in order to search for contentment at this time, and can take advantage of one of the quieter days that has been available for a while. This needn't be a problem, particularly if you demonstrate that for once you are happy to stay still.

4 THURSDAY
Moon Age Day 10   Moon Sign Capricorn

am ....

pm...

Inspiration is now available out in the big wide world, and you won't take much encouragement to pursue it. If the weather is still fairly good, th should also persuade you to get out and about. Concentrating on wor may not be easy, and there is much to be said for simply going and findin yourself some fun.

FRIDAY   *Moon Age Day 11   Moon Sign Capricorn*

....

....

is has potential to be a bountiful time for Gemini, and there is nothing
ong with seeking some assistance with this, particularly at work. For so
ny of you the weekend begins this evening, and putting your feet up
y not appear on your agenda! If travel is planned for tomorrow, why
t get yourself organised tonight?

SATURDAY   *Moon Age Day 12   Moon Sign Aquarius*

....

....

is is probably the very best day of the week for spending time at home
d for doing simple things that satisfy you. You benefit from a deep sense
belonging, and might choose to spend time with family members rather
n with friends. Your sense of give and take has rarely been stronger,
d this helps you to boost the potential of loved ones.

SUNDAY   *Moon Age Day 13   Moon Sign Aquarius*

....

....

eping busy on the domestic scene would be no bad thing, and you
ve scope to make this a very active sort of Sunday. Confirming some
your earlier suspicions, you can get well ahead of the game generally,
d should be able to use intense intuition to assess people and situations.
ok out for love, which could take you by surprise today.

LOVE	MONEY	CAREER	VITALITY	
				+ 5
				+ 4
				+ 3
				+ 2
				+ 1
				- 1
				- 2
				- 3
				- 4
				- 5

8 MONDAY
Moon Age Day 14   Moon Sign Pisc

am ....

pm ....

A higher degree of emotional contentment is within your grasp now, an
some of this may be down to how you respond to the behaviour of other
rather than just your own personality. Once again you are encouraged t
settle for a reasonably quite time, secure in the bosom of your family an
not needing too much else.

9 TUESDAY
Moon Age Day 15   Moon Sign Pisc

am ....

pm...

Around this time your home life continues to be favoured, assisting yo
to make the most of family relationships. In some respects you mig
feel as though you're all fingers and thumbs, but that's something th
happens to Gemini people occasionally. 'More haste, less speed' shou
probably be your motto under current influences.

10 WEDNESDAY
Moon Age Day 16   Moon Sign Ar

am ....

pm...

This is a period during which devoting some time to your own needs c
make all the difference. Trends indicate a slightly quieter interlude th
of late for Gemini, giving you time to think and to plan. Even if the
are plenty of potential invitations on offer, there's nothing wrong wi
watching and waiting for a while.

11 THURSDAY
Moon Age Day 17   Moon Sign Ar

am ....

pm...

You can expect to have your work cut out now, particularly if there a
some really awkward people around and you have to deal with them.
ought to be like water off a duck's back, but you are often more sensit
than you pretend to be. Talking to friends would be a good tonic,
would spending time with someone very close to you.

2 FRIDAY
Moon Age Day 18   Moon Sign Aries

n..

n..

rofessional developments are well highlighted as the working week
omes to a close for many of you. Take the opportunity to bring forward
few plans that have been hatching in your mind, and be willing to rely
n the support of colleagues. You can still afford to be involved in projects
at have to do with your home surroundings.

3 SATURDAY
Moon Age Day 19   Moon Sign Taurus

n..

n..

rends this weekend are geared almost exclusively towards leisure and
easure, so it's a question of finding time to do something that pleases
ou. What is unlikely to impress you is being constantly at the beck and
ll of people who are quite capable of doing things for themselves. It's
ometimes necessary to be a little blunt.

4 SUNDAY
Moon Age Day 20   Moon Sign Taurus

n..

m..

's important today to keep your wits about you and to avoid relying
oo heavily on anyone you don't trust wholeheartedly. Even if this means
onvincing others that you know what you are talking about, this would
e better than making a huge mistake. Instinctive reactions are very
mportant for Gemini at this time.

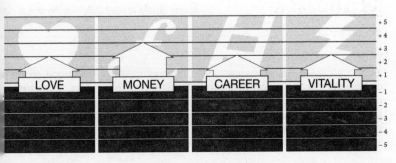

15 MONDAY
Moon Age Day 21   Moon Sign Gemini

am ....

pm ....

Along comes the lunar high and the time is right for action! New incentives seem to be available from all sorts of directions, and you clearly have what it takes to turn heads and to make the best of impressions. If you keep Lady Luck on your side you should be in a favourable position to take the odd chance.

16 TUESDAY
Moon Age Day 22   Moon Sign Gemini

am ....

pm ....

The lunar high acts as a planetary pick-me-up and allows you to make the sort of progress you might feel has sometimes been lacking of late, considering all the domestic trends that have surrounded you. You have what it takes to cruise towards your objectives, and needn't allow yourself to be held back or thwarted as much as has sometimes been the case.

17 WEDNESDAY
Moon Age Day 23   Moon Sign Cancer

am ....

pm ....

Being reliable and doing the right thing is all very well, though you need to remember that this isn't always the way you function best. Try to relax a little and avoid getting yourself into a state about issues you can't alter. By the afternoon a somewhat more relaxed and easy-going approach is definitely possible.

18 THURSDAY
Moon Age Day 24   Moon Sign Cancer

am ....

pm ....

From a professional perspective you have everything you need to be on top form at the moment, and can use this to make the sort of impression that you know is possible. You can't expect everyone to be on your side but you can persuade those who do have a strong bearing on your life to help you when it matters most.

9 FRIDAY

Moon Age Day 25   Moon Sign Cancer

า...

n...

ne strong support you can elicit from those higher up the ladder than u can make all the difference, but if you really want to make the most this you might have to be ready with the compliments. You are not turally obsequious, but on occasions it doesn't do you any harm to say e right things at the right time.

0 SATURDAY

Moon Age Day 26   Moon Sign Leo

า...

n...

e ready to deal with the odd problem in your social life or even in normal endships. This means keeping your finger on the pulse in terms of the y people are really feeling – both about life and about you. There are casions when you can be just a little thoughtless, and you need to make re that this is not one of them.

1 SUNDAY

Moon Age Day 27   Moon Sign Leo

า...

n...

me objectives might now have to be rethought or even scrapped. You n't take everything forward with you into the future, and this may even clude a particular relationship of some sort that has been causing you gnificant trouble. Take steps to ensure that the people you care for the ost remain unaffected by this attitude.

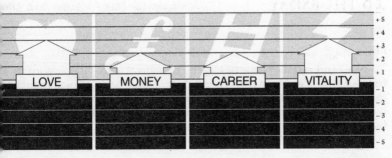

22 MONDAY
Moon Age Day 28   Moon Sign Virgo

am..

pm..

Positive working relationships lie at the heart of your contentment around now. Pursuing happiness at home is all well and good, but if things are not going the way you would wish in a career sense, the picture is incomplete. Some reorganisation of your work life would be no bad thing – and as soon as you can achieve it.

23 TUESDAY
Moon Age Day 29   Moon Sign Virgo

am..

pm..

There are influences around now that assist you to come much more into the social limelight than might have been the case during the last couple of weeks. Your potential popularity is definitely enhanced, and you have what it takes to turn heads wherever you go. Even if the start of the day isn't exactly inspiring, that shouldn't prevent movement later.

24 WEDNESDAY
Moon Age Day 0   Moon Sign Virgo

am..

pm..

Now is the time to make the most of your social desires by mixing quite freely with the sort of people who excite and stimulate you. It's worth making sure that your actions don't inspire jealousy in others. Remember that the things you say to your loved ones should be aimed at bringing you closer to them, rather than further away.

25 THURSDAY
Moon Age Day 1   Moon Sign Libra

am..

pm..

The give and take principle of Gemini remains essential if you want to get on as well as possible at the present time. Don't be too quick to take the initiative, and instead be willing to persuade those around you to accept more of the running of their own lives. An ideal interlude to resolve an old issues that have been on your mind of late.

6 FRIDAY   *Moon Age Day 2   Moon Sign Libra*

ı ....

ı...

...ther than simply believing everything you hear at the moment, it pays ...consider whether some of it is plain wrong. Even if people aren't ...liberately trying to deceive you, perhaps they too have been fooled by ...cumstances. There are good reasons to turn detective in order to get ...the bottom of specific issues that are bothering you.

7 SATURDAY   *Moon Age Day 3   Moon Sign Scorpio*

ı ....

ı...

...atters of intellect come under the spotlight at the moment, encouraging ...u to take up any sort of mental challenge. Getting back into gear after a ...ghtly quieter interlude might be an issue for some Gemini types around ...w, but that needn't stop you from making this a fairly productive and ...teresting sort of day.

8 SUNDAY   *Moon Age Day 4   Moon Sign Scorpio*

ı ....

ı...

...veloping your talent for creativity counts for a great deal under today's ...fluences. It's time to realise that you could well have more going ...r you than you realise, and to recognise your own desire to move to ...eater independence. You have everything you need to be active and ...terprising, and needn't let much hold you back around now.

LOVE	MONEY	CAREER	VITALITY

29 MONDAY
Moon Age Day 5   Moon Sign Sagittari

am ....

pm...

Progress at work is now possible if you can make something out of t
original ideas that are running through your head all the time. Desp
the lunar low, you can afford to opt for a challenge, and shouldn't ta
no for an answer when you know what you want. You can best avc
unnecessary rules and regulations by finding ways around them.

30 TUESDAY
Moon Age Day 6   Moon Sign Sagittari

am ....

pm...

Setbacks can't be ruled out, and if there is a situation you can't avoid, y
need to find ways to use it instead. It's a question of remaining ingenio
and thinking your way out of issues that seem to hold you back. Wh
won't help at this time is knocking your head against a brick wall. Patien
is essential.

1 WEDNESDAY
Moon Age Day 7   Moon Sign Sagittari

am ....

pm...

You might be tempted to show off a little at the beginning of October
not that this is particularly peculiar for Gemini. All the same, there's a ri
that you could give the wrong impression, so it's worth allowing othe
to stand in the limelight, at least for a while. There's no doubt about yo
popularity – but don't milk it!

2 THURSDAY
Moon Age Day 8   Moon Sign Caprico

am ....

pm...

Enjoying personal liberty should be somehow much easier today. Freedo
of expression suits the current planetary influences, and there is much
be said for letting other people know exactly how you feel. Fortunate
you also have astrological trends around at the moment that highlig
your diplomacy and tact.

FRIDAY
Moon Age Day 9   Moon Sign Capricorn

....

....

all means to focus on minor obligations, but don't get carried away
h them. All in all, it's the bigger picture that counts, and so this is an
al time to start casting at least part of your mind far into the future. It
mportant that you get some time to yourself today, and concentrate on
ngs that please only you.

SATURDAY
Moon Age Day 10   Moon Sign Aquarius

....

....

ctical setbacks can't be ruled out today, and these could lead to delays
en it comes to doing things you have planned. Your best approach is to
ow a high degree of patience, because shouting or stamping your feet
nlikely to help. In your friendships with others, you should be willing
show how loyal you can be.

SUNDAY
☿ *Moon Age Day 11   Moon Sign Aquarius*

....

....

is is a period during which you can capitalise on the opportunity to
 something new or unusual. Variety is the spice of life to Gemini, and
ing something that is different from the norm can refresh and revitalise
 day, no matter how tired or worn down you are actually feeling.

LOVE	MONEY	CAREER	VITALITY

+5 +4 +3 +2 +1 −1 −2 −3 −4 −5

Ⅱ

October

2014

YOUR MONTH AT A GLANCE

(+) = Opportunities are around ● = Be on the defensive = Life is pretty ordin

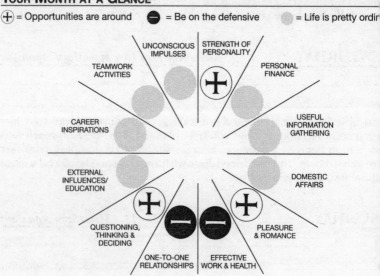

STRENGTH OF PERSONALITY

UNCONSCIOUS IMPULSES

TEAMWORK ACTIVITIES

PERSONAL FINANCE

CAREER INSPIRATIONS

USEFUL INFORMATION GATHERING

EXTERNAL INFLUENCES/ EDUCATION

DOMESTIC AFFAIRS

QUESTIONING, THINKING & DECIDING

PLEASURE & ROMANCE

ONE-TO-ONE RELATIONSHIPS

EFFECTIVE WORK & HEALTH

OCTOBER HIGHS AND LOWS

Here I show you how the rhythms of the Moon will affect you this mon Like the tide, your energies and abilities will rise and fall with its patte When it is above the centre line, go for it, when it is below, you shou be resting.

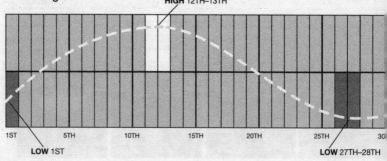

HIGH 12TH–13TH

1ST   5TH   10TH   15TH   20TH   25TH   30

LOW 1ST

LOW 27TH–28TH

MONDAY ☿ *Moon Age Day 12 Moon Sign Pisces*

n ....

n ....

Although it may not be easy today to get your message across to others, both professionally and socially, it should be worth the extra effort. Gemini people who work today can take advantage of better than average potential. You can certainly help your own progress by seeking the sort of support you need throughout your active hours.

TUESDAY ☿ *Moon Age Day 13 Moon Sign Pisces*

n ....

n ....

Relationships are particularly favoured, even if you don't have the time to explore them during the first half of today. This period works best if you keep yourself busy, and skipping from one task to the next could well be a natural aspect of life now. All in all, you have scope to make this a generally happy and productive day.

WEDNESDAY ☿ *Moon Age Day 14 Moon Sign Aries*

n ....

n ....

You have a great deal to gain from the atmosphere at home, and for this reason you may decide to spend less time on practical and professional matters right now. Try to relax and enjoy whatever today has to offer. Although the year is growing older, you can still revel in outdoor activities.

THURSDAY ☿ *Moon Age Day 15 Moon Sign Aries*

n ....

n ....

There are advantageous situations available today, particularly if you are a working Gemini. Don't be put off by people who always seem to find problems in any situation, and be sure that you put all your effort into new plans and schemes. Be prepared to turn detective if you find the behaviour of some friends rather a puzzle.

129

10 FRIDAY ☿ *Moon Age Day 16   Moon Sign Taur*

am...

pm...

Romance and social matters have the potential to keep you smiling no
and you are in a position to turn this into a happy-go-lucky sort of d
– just the kind that is meat and drink to Gemini. It's worth looking f
a chance to show those close to you just how important they are. Und
current trends, this could provoke an interesting response.

11 SATURDAY ☿ *Moon Age Day 17   Moon Sign Taur*

am...

pm...

You may feel that your influence over everyday matters is somewh
limited, but only for today. The reason is that the Moon is in your so
twelfth house, bringing an element of uncertainty and encouraging yo
to focus on some deep thoughts. If the attitude of those around yo
seems positive, why not listen to what they have to say?

12 SUNDAY ☿ *Moon Age Day 18   Moon Sign Gemi*

am...

pm...

A continuing phase of rewarding times is on offer, even if this doesn
seem to be the case early on today. The Moon moves into your zodi
sign, bringing the lunar high, and from around lunchtime on you ha
what it takes to make some useful progress. You can afford to take t
odd chance and to push your luck, especially at work.

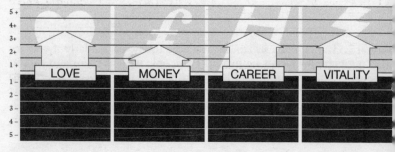

3 MONDAY ☿ *Moon Age Day 19   Moon Sign Gemini*

n...

n...

nergy levels remain highlighted, and you should realise that you can
ove forward with something you are trying to achieve around this time.
ur enterprising approach should mean you are good to know, and you
ight even like yourself better than has been the case for a week or two.
ll the same, don't waste time looking in the mirror – activity is the key!

4 TUESDAY ☿ *Moon Age Day 20   Moon Sign Cancer*

n...

n...

eing noticed is what matters for now – pure and simple. Gemini is no
rinking violet at the best of times, but right now you have an opportunity
 take centre stage in any activity or plan that takes your fancy. Part of
is is getting others to listen to your thoughts and opinions. Just make
re that you have some interesting things to say.

5 WEDNESDAY ☿ *Moon Age Day 21   Moon Sign Cancer*

n...

n...

you keep up your accustomed high profile today, you ought to be able
 make some progress. There are a couple of quieter days ahead of you,
 it's worth getting things out of the way now. Even if you feel you are
edged in by everyday routines, you needn't allow these to prevent you
om pushing forward generally.

6 THURSDAY ☿ *Moon Age Day 22   Moon Sign Cancer*

n...

n...

day to capitalise on a potential winning streak as far as your work is
oncerned, so don't miss out on any opportunity to get ahead. This
ight include seeking support from colleagues, and making the most of
e attention you can attract from the right sort of people. Confidence is
ell starred, and excitement is self-made.

17 FRIDAY ☿ *Moon Age Day 23   Moon Sign Leo*

am...

pm...

It's worth taking plenty of time to make up your mind about issues at the
moment, so the instant decision-making of Gemini could well be out of
the window ahead of the weekend. Personal plans are subject to change
and you need to show a very flexible and even an off-hand approach if you
want to seem cool in the eyes of others.

18 SATURDAY ☿ *Moon Age Day 24   Moon Sign Leo*

am...

pm...

This would be an ideal interlude to focus on issues from the past, though
this time you should be ready to deal with them properly. Don't ignore
the needs of family members, especially those who seem to be subdued at
present. The attitude of your partner is also important, and a good chat
would probably work wonders.

19 SUNDAY ☿ *Moon Age Day 25   Moon Sign Virgo*

am...

pm...

You reach a definite peak as far as communications generally are concerned.
This is definitely a favourable day to get your message across and to let
those around you know that you are open to negotiation. Don't be held
back by the odd peculiar type. It's up to you to decide whether some
people should simply be ignored at present.

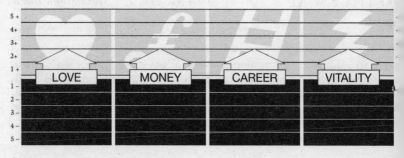

0 MONDAY ☿ *Moon Age Day 26   Moon Sign Virgo*

n ....

n ....

ur emotional state can have a bearing on the decisions you are likely to
e making around this time. Confidence could be starting to grow, but
r the moment there's nothing wrong with allowing others to make at
ast some of the running. Romance is highlighted for some, but even
ere it is possible you will encounter obstacles.

1 TUESDAY ☿ *Moon Age Day 27   Moon Sign Virgo*

n ....

n ....

sserting yourself among friends shouldn't present any sort of problem
 you at present. However, the slightly shyer side of your nature is
mphasised when it comes to dealing with strangers. Fortunately, such a
riod is never going to last long for gregarious and intrepid Gemini. It's
 to you to make the best of all situations today.

2 WEDNESDAY ☿ *Moon Age Day 28   Moon Sign Libra*

n ....

n ....

his is a day to push towards career success. There are gains to be made
om convincing people to listen to what you have to say and persuading
em to follow your lead. Being told what to do is unlikely to appeal at
e moment, but a little discretion is very important. Avoid getting on
e wrong side of superiors.

3 THURSDAY ☿ *Moon Age Day 0   Moon Sign Libra*

n ....

n ....

ny work that involves you coming into direct co-operation with others
 extremely well highlighted around now. You probably won't want to
 it alone in any case, and can gain a great deal by being part of a team.
lthough Gemini sometimes has a dominant streak, this needn't be the
se today.

24 FRIDAY ☿ *Moon Age Day 1 Moon Sign Scorp*

am...

pm...

When it comes to practical matters you should be right on the ball at th
moment. You have what it takes to see clear through to the heart of ju
about any matter, and will be able to show that penetrating insight th
occasionally sets you apart. Don't be too quick to judge the actions
intentions of a friend.

25 SATURDAY ☿ *Moon Age Day 2 Moon Sign Scorp*

am...

pm...

Getting your own way with others is really not the issue this weekend, b
rather going with the flow. You can gain a great deal by simply accepti
that those around you have opinions of their own. It wouldn't hurt at
to let someone feel as though they are winning for once, and you have
chance to gain friends as a result.

26 SUNDAY *Moon Age Day 3 Moon Sign Scorp*

am...

pm...

It is possible that emotional aspects of your life are something you simp
cannot avoid looking at today. Your willingness to help others with the
difficulties counts for a great deal under current influences. Certainty
the order of the day at work, though that doesn't mean you can't list
to an alternative point of view.

5 +			
4 +			
3 +			
2 +			
1 +			
LOVE	MONEY	CAREER	VITALITY
1 −			
2 −			
3 −			
4 −			
5 −			

27 MONDAY
Moon Age Day 4   Moon Sign Sagittarius

m ....

m ....

It might be sensible to allow others to make the decisions for the moment. The lunar low this month indicates a tendency for you to shy away from issues, which is really unusual for Gemini. These trends only last a very short time, but until you can make more progress, there's much to be said for choosing to put your feet up and relax.

28 TUESDAY
Moon Age Day 5   Moon Sign Sagittarius

m ....

m ....

Even if direct inspiration is lacking, you can take advantage of a genuine sixth sense when it matters the most. Following your intuition should now allow you to ride out the worst of the lunar low, almost without realising what's happening. Your personality is able to blossom all the more when you are surrounded by essentially dull people.

29 WEDNESDAY
Moon Age Day 6   Moon Sign Capricorn

m ....

m ....

Though personal ambitions should be on course at present, you would be wise not to overstep the mark and expect too much from others. A little diplomacy goes a long way, particularly where your partner is concerned. Beware any tendency to be domineering, particularly when it comes to dealing with certain quieter individuals.

30 THURSDAY
Moon Age Day 7   Moon Sign Capricorn

m ....

m ....

If you feel that your love life is somewhat in the doldrums, now is the time to do something about the situation. Simply telling your partner just how important they are to you can work wonders, and a small token of your feelings may also help. You know how much you care, but this would be an ideal opportunity to demonstrate the fact.

31 FRIDAY
Moon Age Day 8   Moon Sign Aquari

am ....

pm ....

Your personal life is now well accented, and you can ensure that roman
figures strongly, mainly as a result of the effort you have been puttin
in over recent days. Today works best if you can allow some situatio
to look after themselves, especially at work, and don't try to contr
everything on your own.

1 SATURDAY
Moon Age Day 9   Moon Sign Aquari

am ....

pm ....

Everyone needs to retreat from the world now and again, and th
weekend should offer Gemini the perfect opportunity to do so. Tren
highlight a natural inclination to stick to those people with whom you fe
most comfortable. On the way you can offer the love and support that
so much appreciated by family and close friends.

2 SUNDAY
Moon Age Day 10   Moon Sign Pisc

am ....

pm ....

Social life and group ventures remain central themes in your life, ar
could assist you to discover that you have friends you never dream
about. What really makes the difference now is how diplomatic you a
capable of being. Getting what you want from life should be well with
your grasp under present influences.

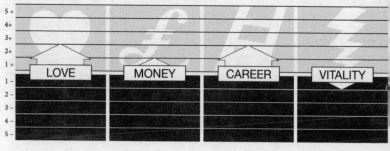

November
2014

UR MONTH AT A GLANCE

= Opportunities are around ● = Be on the defensive ● = Life is pretty ordinary

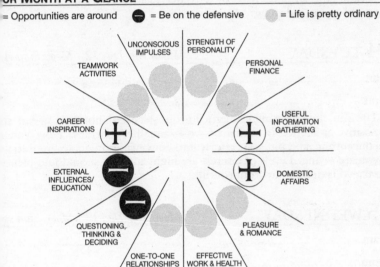

UNCONSCIOUS IMPULSES

STRENGTH OF PERSONALITY

TEAMWORK ACTIVITIES

PERSONAL FINANCE

CAREER INSPIRATIONS

USEFUL INFORMATION GATHERING

EXTERNAL INFLUENCES/ EDUCATION

DOMESTIC AFFAIRS

QUESTIONING, THINKING & DECIDING

PLEASURE & ROMANCE

ONE-TO-ONE RELATIONSHIPS

EFFECTIVE WORK & HEALTH

OVEMBER HIGHS AND LOWS

re I show you how the rhythms of the Moon will affect you this month.
e the tide, your energies and abilities will rise and fall with its pattern.
nen it is above the centre line, go for it, when it is below, you should
resting.

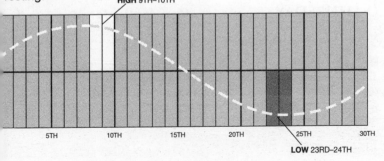

HIGH 9TH–10TH

5TH 10TH 15TH 20TH 25TH 30TH

LOW 23RD–24TH

3 MONDAY
Moon Age Day 11   Moon Sign Pi

am ....

pm ....

Any plans to make money at the moment are probably best left on ho
Your instinct for such matters is not enhanced by current planetary tren
and you are encouraged to turn your mind to less practical matt
Seeking the sound advice of an older relative or friend at some st
would be no bad thing.

4 TUESDAY
Moon Age Day 12   Moon Sign A

am ....

pm ....

The Sun, now showing its mettle in your solar sixth house, is an extrem
positive influence in terms of work and life generally. Now you
concentrate, and put your efforts into convincing others to listen to w
you are saying. Levels of interest are high, and you should find plenty
take your mind away from routine.

5 WEDNESDAY
Moon Age Day 13   Moon Sign A

am ....

pm ....

Better financial propositions are there for the taking, but you need to
sure that you are attentive enough to recognise them. Concentration
keyword at present, and remains so until after the weekend. Your me
processes are to the fore, and you have everything you need to att
plenty of attention from others.

6 THURSDAY
Moon Age Day 14   Moon Sign Tau

am ....

pm ....

This is an ideal time to be acting on new opportunities that are availa
to you. There are trends about that might also affect your powers
concentration, so make sure you keep your wits about you. On a posi
note, you shouldn't have any trouble finding something to do today.

FRIDAY   *Moon Age Day 15   Moon Sign Taurus*

....

....

e Moon does you no favours at all now as it moves into your solar
elfth house. This indicates a rather more introspective and even
otional phase than has been the case for the last few days, and your
st response is to slow down somewhat. Even if you know what you
nt from life, it may be difficult to get it today.

SATURDAY   *Moon Age Day 16   Moon Sign Taurus*

....

....

u need to capitalise on the support you can elicit from influential
ures at this time, a situation that offers new opportunities and allows
u to brighten things up no end at work. This would be a favourable
e to consider looking for a new job or to think in terms of taking on
ferent responsibilities.

SUNDAY   *Moon Age Day 17   Moon Sign Gemini*

....

....

is period coincides with a new burst of energy and allows you to look at
ngs afresh. Romance has a natural part to play in life during this lunar
h, and unattached Gemini people can take advantage of this in their
rch for new love. There can be something deeply sensual about today,
d you should revel in the popularity you can achieve.

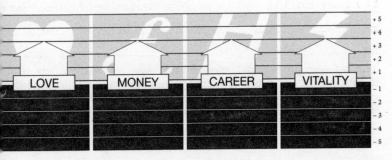

10 MONDAY
Moon Age Day 18   Moon Sign Gem

am ....

pm ....

A day during which you have everything you need to get more or ▌
what you want from life. You needn't hold back at all, and should f▌
that a little cheek really does go a long way. Creative potential is extrem▌
well accented, but not half as noteworthy as your popularity. This ▌
great time to socialise.

11 TUESDAY
Moon Age Day 19   Moon Sign Can

am ....

pm ....

A spirit of equality predominates today, which should make it easy for y▌
to associate with just about anyone. Even if you are mixing with comp▌
that has seemed awkward before, you can now begin to shine noticea▌
There's no need to look up to others – or down on them for that mat▌
This is a sure sign of the egalitarian qualities of Gemini.

12 WEDNESDAY
Moon Age Day 20   Moon Sign Can

am ....

pm ....

Once again, the atmosphere in social settings is favourable, and it's ti▌
to show just how lively Gemini can be. Although those around y▌
might prove to be rather cautious in their approach to life, this doe▌
necessarily have to be true of you. Be ready to deal with problems wh▌
trying to reconcile your own needs with those of family members.

13 THURSDAY
Moon Age Day 21   Moon Sign ▌

am ....

pm ....

Joint finances are worth a second look now, and there is much to ▌
said for spending a few hours sorting out such things. This shouldn't ▌
too much of a struggle, because there are strong family trends aroun▌
present and a genuine need to be in the company of your partner or oth▌
family members.

4 FRIDAY
Moon Age Day 22   Moon Sign Leo

....

....

...st career initiatives are now well starred, though there may be other ...as of life that prove to be significantly less fulfilling. Avoid causing ...nfusion at work by stating very clearly what you mean, and be ready to ... suade any reluctant associates to take the sort of chances that come as ...ond nature to you.

5 SATURDAY
Moon Age Day 23   Moon Sign Leo

....

....

... gotiations of almost any sort are now favoured, and today could also ... an ideal opportunity for getting together with friends. A sensible view ...life works best for Gemini at the moment, and you can also gain some ...ra respect by showing plenty of humility. In social settings your silver ...gue really helps.

6 SUNDAY
Moon Age Day 24   Moon Sign Virgo

....

....

...e desire to feel busy is emphasised by current planetary influences, ... couraging you to find plenty of things to do from the time you get ... until the moment you crawl back into bed again. There's nothing ...ticularly strange about that for Gemini, and it can certainly help you ... make progress. However, you ought to find at least a few moments to ...ditate.

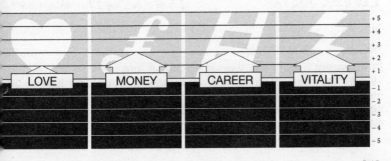

17 MONDAY
Moon Age Day 25   Moon Sign Vi

am ....

pm...

Looking for something special to do that will blow the cobwebs aw
and make you feel more alive? Then join the rest of the people be
under your zodiac sign, for whom today offers great scope for stimulat
pursuits. Your compassion for other people is also highlighted, and t
itself might be enough to keep you busy for most of today.

18 TUESDAY
Moon Age Day 26   Moon Sign Li

am ....

pm...

The present phase tends to give you a chance to focus your mind
domestic matters. Perhaps you are securing your castle for the forthcom
winter, or maybe worrying about any younger family members wh
behaviour is causing concern. If you can treat all situations with humo
they are certainly likely to seem less important.

19 WEDNESDAY
Moon Age Day 27   Moon Sign Li

am ....

pm...

Even if you feel slightly insecure in one or two ways, in the main y
should be able to get things running fairly smoothly. Your ruling plar
Mercury, is presently very supportive as far as personal and roman
trends are concerned. Be ready to seek out some interesting people la
in the day, and to relish what they have to offer.

20 THURSDAY
Moon Age Day 28   Moon Sign Li

am ....

pm...

It may seem natural today to spend time trying to please others, thou
despite your best efforts it won't always work. You might have to acc
that some people are quite happy being miserable, and that there is v
little you can do about it. Sometimes it's easier to stick with close frien
who are less likely to cause you any problems.

1 FRIDAY
Moon Age Day 29   Moon Sign Scorpio

n...

n...

eware of falling prey to the manipulative tendencies of those around
ou, and in particular, avoid reacting to emotional blackmail. You need
 be a little hard in your dealings with others, especially if you feel that
ey are somehow taking you for a ride. Routines might seem tedious,
it they work for you right now.

2 SATURDAY
Moon Age Day 0   Moon Sign Scorpio

n...

n...

our ability to attract life's little pleasures is assisted by present astrological
ends, and you shouldn't have to work very hard in order to get other
ople on your side. Romance looks especially well marked, and this
ould be an ideal time to take advantage of all the affection that is on
fer for you when it matters the most.

3 SUNDAY
Moon Age Day 1   Moon Sign Sagittarius

n...

n...

ith the lunar low now around, taking on anything new is not particularly
commended for the next two or three days. There are good reasons to
mply stand and stare for a while, and maybe get some fresh air before
e cold weather begins to set in. This is not an auspicious time to take
ances of any sort.

LOVE	MONEY	CAREER	VITALITY

24 MONDAY
Moon Age Day 2   Moon Sign Sagittari

am ....

pm ....

Be prepared to deal with personal setbacks and to approach life as stead as you can. Rather than getting involved in too many new ventures, i worth seeking out, and taking notice of, the sound advice that is availab around you. You have what it takes to water down the influence of t lunar low this month using the support you gain from all sides.

25 TUESDAY
Moon Age Day 3   Moon Sign Capricor

am ....

pm ....

Your powers of attraction are now clearly at a peak and you need make the most of this fact. It's time to call in favours and to ask for th special help that can make all the difference to something you have be planning. Finances are favoured for Gemini, even if you have to spe more than expected right now.

26 WEDNESDAY
Moon Age Day 4   Moon Sign Capricor

am ....

pm ....

This is a fantastic day to make sure you are around your favour people. There are gains to be made on the financial front and a genera optimistic attitude prevails. This is Gemini at its brightest and best, a it's something that everyone likes to see. This is especially true in the ca of your partner or someone else you hold dear.

27 THURSDAY
Moon Age Day 5   Moon Sign Aquari

am ....

pm ....

There are signs that you soak up environmental influences like a spon under present trends, and your sensitivity to others has rarely been bett Confidence remains especially highlighted, and you have what it takes overturn obstacles that have been around for quite some time. Make t most of assistance you can elicit from friends.

8 FRIDAY
Moon Age Day 6   Moon Sign Aquarius

n...

n...

ealing with personal problems at the moment means grasping the nettle
d being especially firm. Being too sensitive won't work as well, and
ere is much to be said for saying how you really feel. There are some
ins to be made on the financial front, even if you aren't particularly
ying to do so.

9 SATURDAY
Moon Age Day 7   Moon Sign Pisces

n...

n...

stead of taking everything you hear as being the truth today, bear
mind that not everyone may be completely reliable in what they are
ying. You need a hefty pinch of salt and the utilisation of your own
agination and common sense. Gemini should still be able to see the
nny side of life, and this in itself turns out to be very important.

0 SUNDAY
Moon Age Day 8   Moon Sign Pisces

n...

n...

may seem important now to try to get to the root of certain matters
at have been on your mind for some time. That's all very well, though
aybe if you relaxed more you would find the answers you seek, because
ey are unlikely to come if you are worrying all the time. Be ready to
ake the most of more positive times to come.

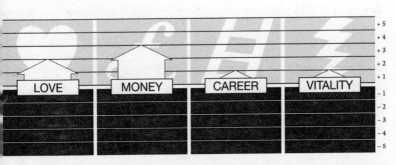

II December
2014

YOUR MONTH AT A GLANCE

$\oplus$ = Opportunities are around $\ominus$ = Be on the defensive   ⬤ = Life is pretty ordin

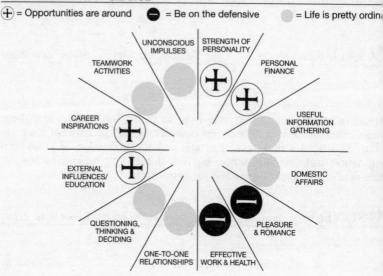

DECEMBER HIGHS AND LOWS

Here I show you how the rhythms of the Moon will affect you this mont Like the tide, your energies and abilities will rise and fall with its patter When it is above the centre line, go for it, when it is below, you shou be resting.

HIGH 6TH–7TH

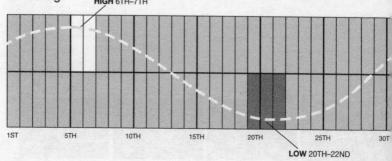

LOW 20TH–22ND

MONDAY
Moon Age Day 9   Moon Sign Pisces

....

....

is is a marvellous period for twosomes, and an ideal time for seeking ppiness in the arms of your lover. The present position of the Sun makes ossible for you to fully express yourself, and to attract some incredible mpliments from those around you. Why not do an extra bit of work lay in order to save time later?

TUESDAY
Moon Age Day 10   Moon Sign Aries

....

....

terms of your career you have everything you need to shine now, and : same is true if you are presently involved in any form of education. rt of this is making sure you are aware of the people who can do you : greatest favours at this stage of the month. Turning away any offers of dness would probably be a short-sighted move.

WEDNESDAY
Moon Age Day 11   Moon Sign Aries

....

....

ose ties may not bring out the best in you right now, and you may cide you'd be better off spending time with casual friends. There is om to change your mind at work but less flexibility in home-based tters. Be prepared to deal with the demands of other people. This ght even mean being in three places at once!

THURSDAY
Moon Age Day 12   Moon Sign Taurus

....

....

pport could be available where finances are concerned, even if this is ly in an advisory sense. A slight reversal in fortunes is possible during s part of the week, but any disappointments needn't last for very long. u can't expect everything to go quite as well as you would wish, though naining generally cheerful should help.

5 FRIDAY
Moon Age Day 13   Moon Sign Tau

am ....

pm...

This has potential to be one of the best days of the month for maki
yourself as visible as you can. As a result, you are encouraged to fo
your attention on your appearance, and to shine for all you are worth.
personal attachments, you would be wise to avoid the little green-ey
monster of jealousy.

6 SATURDAY
Moon Age Day 14   Moon Sign Gem

am ....

pm...

You have what it takes to talk anyone into anything right now. The f
is that when Gemini is working at its best, it can overcome any obstac
that are in view. The lunar high is a time to tap into the assistance y
have been seeking, particularly at work, and to take advantage of wl
Lady Luck has to offer.

7 SUNDAY
Moon Age Day 15   Moon Sign Gem

am ....

pm...

It's time to put yourself in the right place at the best possible time. Ma
the most of the favourable trends that are available, and be bold in yc
approach to others, especially at work. Be prepared to deal with a
contradictions that you encounter, preferably as you go along. In t
main, life should be going your way.

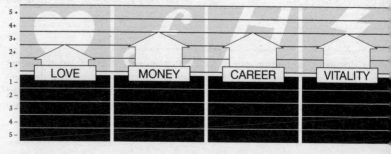

MONDAY　　　　*Moon Age Day 16　Moon Sign Cancer*

n ....

n ....

ans that are presently on the boil can be given an extra boost, and there ould be little to stop you on your personal quest to make the sort of lash that can get you noticed. There are quite a few people around at is time who can be persuaded to support you. Take opportunities as and hen they arise.

TUESDAY　　　　*Moon Age Day 17　Moon Sign Cancer*

n ....

n ....

a financial sense, this is a time that lends itself to short-term bonuses. ou may as well enjoy the gains while they last, though that doesn't ecessarily mean you'll be hanging on to your cash. You do have the ance to get ahead in something that is quite important to you, and edn't be tardy when it comes to having your say.

0 WEDNESDAY　　　　*Moon Age Day 18　Moon Sign Cancer*

n ....

n ....

he emphasis today is on keeping everyday life running fairly smoothly, d finding plenty of time for enjoyment, which is what is needed at is time of year. If the approach of Christmas becomes a bore, then it ill probably be more difficult to enjoy it. There's nothing wrong with aintaining a sense of childlike excitement.

1 THURSDAY　　　　*Moon Age Day 19　Moon Sign Leo*

n ....

n ....

is the domestic arena that offers the best chance of interest and happiness day. Although you still have the ability to make gains at work, bear in ind that the actions or ideas of colleagues can sometimes take the gilt f the gingerbread. When work is out of the way, the emphasis should e on relaxation.

12 FRIDAY
Moon Age Day 20   Moon Sign L...

am...

pm...

Trends indicate a slightly more judgemental attitude today than is usu...
for your zodiac sign. Whether this turns out to be a good thing or n...
really depends on the evidence you have to hand. Perhaps it would ...
better if you started out in each case expecting situations and people ...
assist rather than to hinder you.

13 SATURDAY
Moon Age Day 21   Moon Sign Vir...

am...

pm...

Ups and downs are part of what today has to offer, but whether or n...
you have a good time is more or less solely tied to your attitude. There ...
a slight tendency to feel trapped, and fighting as hard as you can to fr...
yourself is a natural reaction. The spotlight is once again on your burnin...
need to escape.

14 SUNDAY
Moon Age Day 22   Moon Sign Vir...

am...

pm...

This is a day during which you are encouraged to emphasise the practic...
qualities you possess. Be ready to welcome characters into your life at th...
time, and give yourself a treat by taking time away from jobs you hat...
Although it's getting late in the year, travel is well starred for Gemini ...
this time.

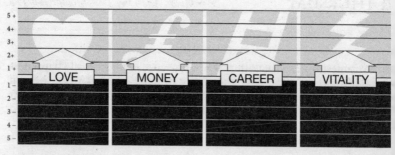

5 MONDAY
Moon Age Day 23   Moon Sign Virgo

n ....

n ....

our social life and one-to-one relationships are of equal importance at
the start of this working week, so why not ditch those jobs you hate
and simply set out to have a good time? It's important for Gemini to
recognise the potential for exciting new friendships, and this is also an
ideal interlude for trying to please as many people as possible.

6 TUESDAY
Moon Age Day 24   Moon Sign Libra

n ....

n ....

Make the most of the scope you have for advancement in your life
generally, and let your light shine, especially in a social sense. It might
be only just occurring to you that Christmas is in view, and that means a
great many preparations. This week offers you the chance to make some
of them.

7 WEDNESDAY
Moon Age Day 25   Moon Sign Libra

n ....

n ....

Trends encourage some strong opinions, and even if nobody is stopping
you from expressing these, it's worth tempering this tendency with a little
diplomacy. You can get your own way far better by approaching others
gently than by trying to bulldoze people in a way they could tend to
resent. Tact is the key to progress now.

8 THURSDAY
Moon Age Day 26   Moon Sign Scorpio

n ....

n ....

Business and practical matters now count for a great deal. This is a
favourable time to make new contacts – particularly ones that will be
important for a long time to come. Socially speaking you have what it
takes to be on top form, and it's up to you to show the world what a
Gemini is really like.

19 FRIDAY
Moon Age Day 27   Moon Sign Scorp

am...

pm...

Financial matters can benefit from some fortunate influences toda assisting you to make more progress than you expected. Rather th taking offence at the things other people say, bear in mind that th might not mean any harm. Routines that need to be dealt with ahead Christmas itself could prove irksome, but they may still be necessary.

20 SATURDAY
Moon Age Day 28   Moon Sign Sagittari

am...

pm...

Disappointments are possible in social matters as the lunar low arriv particularly if you are expecting more from others than they are willing offer. There is much to be said for concentrating instead on your wor which has more potential for success at present. By the evening, relaxatio is the name of the game!

21 SUNDAY
Moon Age Day 29   Moon Sign Sagittari

am...

pm...

Although the lunar low does little to lift your spirits or boost your gene vitality, believe it or not you can still make this a terrific day. The less yo expect, the greater the rewards when things do go your way. The secr now is to keep it light and simple and not to be brought low by incident issues that don't matter at all.

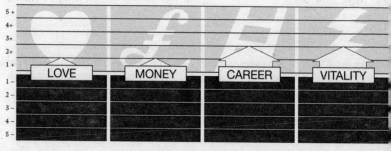

22 MONDAY
Moon Age Day 0   Moon Sign Sagittarius

m ....

m ....

There might be a kind of see-sawing today between your personal desires and the things you know you should be doing for others. It can sometimes feel intimidating to have to deal with the demands and expectations that you are facing, but using your common sense can make all the difference now.

23 TUESDAY
Moon Age Day 1   Moon Sign Capricorn

m ....

m ....

You can capitalise on some luck now in practical matters, and should be making the most of the support offered by the present position of Venus in your solar chart. Today is an opportunity to seek an upward turn in personal attachments, and romance could figure strongly in your life as a whole. Family relationships may also begin to look a good deal better.

24 WEDNESDAY
Moon Age Day 2   Moon Sign Capricorn

m ....

m ....

This has potential to be a particularly enjoyable Christmas Eve in almost every respect. Trends indicate an urge to travel, and this may give you the excuse you need to visit relatives or friends. Although you can really have fun, an element of restlessness is also possible. Keeping on the move is the order of the day.

25 THURSDAY
Moon Age Day 3   Moon Sign Aquarius

m ....

m ....

You can afford to be a typical Gemini at present, and that could make this a very chatty Christmas Day! It's a question of finding something kind to say to everyone, and perhaps even deciding that this is the time to bury a hatchet once and for all. Travel is indicated for later in the day, and is well highlighted in your solar chart.

26 FRIDAY
Moon Age Day 4   Moon Sign Aquariu

am...

pm...

The focus right now is on your search for ease and comfort, so this ma
not be a particularly rip-roaring sort of Boxing Day. With a great desire t
put others at their ease, you need to show that you are charming to kno
and that you can lift the spirits of others, especially anyone who has bee
down in the dumps of late.

27 SATURDAY
Moon Age Day 5   Moon Sign Pisc

am...

pm...

Go full steam ahead with your dreams and schemes today and don't l
anything stand in your way. Positive thinking can work wonders, and
you show how charming and determined you can be, you can persuad
others to fall in with your plans. You don't need to argue with anyone a
the moment because you are clearly in charge of most situations.

28 SUNDAY
Moon Age Day 6   Moon Sign Pisc

am...

pm...

Emotional links you share with others are particularly well marked at th
present time, making this an ideal interlude for family activities. A desir
to get on well in the outside world is all very well, though this might b
tricky today. Traditionally, Sunday is said to be a day of rest. Take note c
this fact and make this a steady sort of day.

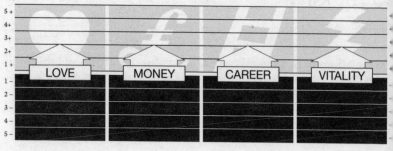

29 MONDAY
Moon Age Day 7   Moon Sign Aries

n...

m..

lucky financial phase is now on offer, and this brings a period during
hich you have scope to spend rather than save. Perhaps you have your
ghts set on the post-Christmas sales, and on something you have been
oveting for quite some time. The gadget freaks among you should really
e in their element now!

30 TUESDAY
Moon Age Day 8   Moon Sign Aries

n...

m..

n social gatherings you now have what it takes to shine and to give your
est in most situations. Be prepared to deal with any awkward people
ou encounter, which could even include family members. Taking such
tuations in your stride means bringing a dose of warmth and humour to
most any situation.

31 WEDNESDAY
Moon Age Day 9   Moon Sign Taurus

n...

m..

his is a time when you are encouraged to suspend certain activities, in
avour of simply soaking up the celebration that goes with the end of a
ear. Even if your energy levels are not quite what you would wish, that
eedn't stop you from pushing the boat out in whatever way you choose
s midnight approaches.

RISING SIGNS FOR GEMINI

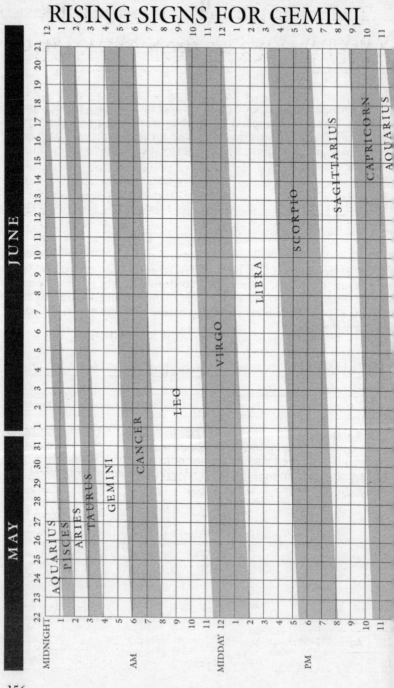

THE ZODIAC, PLANETS AND CORRESPONDENCES

The Earth revolves around the Sun once every calendar year, so when viewed from Earth the Sun appears in a different part of the sky as the year progresses. In astrology, these parts of the sky are divided into the signs of the zodiac and this means that the signs are organised in a circle. The circle begins with Aries and ends with Pisces.

Taking the zodiac sign as a starting point, astrologers then work with all the positions of planets, stars and many other factors to calculate horoscopes and birth charts and tell us what the stars have in store for us.

The table below shows the planets and Elements for each of the signs of the zodiac. Each sign belongs to one of the four Elements: Fire, Air, Earth or Water. Fire signs are creative and enthusiastic; Air signs are mentally active and thoughtful; Earth signs are constructive and practical; Water signs are emotional and have strong feelings.

It also shows the metals and gemstones associated with, or corresponding with, each sign. The correspondence is made when a metal or stone possesses properties that are held in common with a particular sign of the zodiac.

Finally, the table shows the opposite of each star sign – this is the opposite sign in the astrological circle.

Placed	Sign	Symbol	Element	Planet	Metal	Stone	Opposite
1	Aries	Ram	Fire	Mars	Iron	Bloodstone	Libra
2	Taurus	Bull	Earth	Venus	Copper	Sapphire	Scorpio
3	Gemini	Twins	Air	Mercury	Mercury	Tiger's Eye	Sagittarius
4	Cancer	Crab	Water	Moon	Silver	Pearl	Capricorn
5	Leo	Lion	Fire	Sun	Gold	Ruby	Aquarius
6	Virgo	Maiden	Earth	Mercury	Mercury	Sardonyx	Pisces
7	Libra	Scales	Air	Venus	Copper	Sapphire	Aries
8	Scorpio	Scorpion	Water	Pluto	Plutonium	Jasper	Taurus
9	Sagittarius	Archer	Fire	Jupiter	Tin	Topaz	Gemini
10	Capricorn	Goat	Earth	Saturn	Lead	Black Onyx	Cancer
11	Aquarius	Waterbearer	Air	Uranus	Uranium	Amethyst	Leo
12	Pisces	Fishes	Water	Neptune	Tin	Moonstone	Virgo